LISTEN OR DIE

LISTEN OR DIE

40 LESSONS

THAT TURN CUSTOMER FEEDBACK

INTO GOLD

SEAN McDADE, PhD

LIONCREST
PUBLISHING

LISTEN OR DIE
40 Lessons That Turn Customer Feedback into Gold

ISBN 978-1-5445-1081-1 *Hardcover*
      978-1-5445-1079-8 *Paperback*
      978-1-5445-1080-4 *Ebook*

The book is dedicated to the people who deliver great experiences to customers every day. These CX heroes make the world a better place. Thank you for everything you do.

CONTENTS

SECTION THREE: ASK FOR HELP

SECTION FOUR: BUILD A GREAT SURVEY

SECTION FIVE: OPERATIONALIZING VOC

ACKNOWLEDGMENTS

This book would not have been possible without the amazing, incredible team at PeopleMetrics. The 40 lessons in this book are not original ideas by any means, but from what I have learned from these incredible professionals and our clients. In particular, I want to thank Reshma Bennur for her ideas, intellect, and encouragement to write this book. You are the ultimate professional. The customer experience team at PeopleMetrics sat through numerous brainstorming sessions on this book that had a huge influence—thank you to Alyssa Tombler, Audrey Squaresky, Kirk Lohbauer, Rob Farina, and Steve Lakawicz. You all are the best! Madeline Good, your help throughout this book-writing process has been invaluable, and this book would not be done without you. I owe you big time! Bryan Grimes, you made the CRM integration lesson so much better and made me sound smart. Scott Lohbauer, your input was vital to the text analytics and machine learning lessons. Thank you both! David Rode and Reshma, thank you for the thorough review of the manuscript; I know that is a thankless task. I really appreciate it! Pooya Pourak, John Lamanna, and Matt Muscella, thank you for putting up with my never-ending requests for images and diagrams; your patience and awesomeness are duly noted! Kate Feather, many of the ideas in this book were based on our conversations over the years; thank you for your passion for CX and intellectual curiosity! In particular, the lesson on the prospect experience would not exist without your great work.

I also want to thank PeopleMetrics' clients who made the content in the book possible. It's an honor to work with all of you and be a small part of helping you deliver exceptional customer experiences every day. In particular, I would like to thank the handful of clients that I have personally worked closely with over the years that have shape the lessons in this book: Signature Flight Support, Wyndham Vacation Ownership, Mandarin Oriental Hotel Group, C Spire, Service Inspired Restaurants, Crowe, and Windstream Communications. I am in awe of your dedication to your customers and clients.

Finally, I would like to thank my family for putting up with me chomping at the keyboard many nights and weekends over the past year. Natalia, Benjamin, and Henry, thank you from the bottom of my heart.

INTRODUCTION

Every time your customer interacts with your company, their experience will ultimately decide what they will do in the future. Think of it as each customer having a bank account full of experiences. Delivering a great customer experience is like making a deposit for a rainy day—that customer may forgive a mistake or two based on the goodwill you built up over time. But a bad experience is the opposite. It's like a large withdrawal from the bank account, and eventually, if there are enough withdrawals, you will not have that customer any longer. And that customer may very well share their disappointing experience with their friends and even the world via social media.

What's your experiential account balance with each of your customers? How do you know? Have you asked them?

I wrote this book because I get a lot of questions from

customer experience (CX) professionals on the best way to create a customer listening program that will deliver business results, especially reduced churn, better social reviews, and increased top-line revenue.

I have sat in on countless meetings with prospects or clients asking similar questions:

How do I get leadership buy-in for Voice of the Customer (VoC)? How do I increase my response rate? Is NPS the right measure for us? How do I improve NPS? How do I get our people to understand and regularly act on customer feedback? How do I use customer feedback and better customer experiences to really drive my business results?

I always refer folks to the great book by Harley Manning and Kerry Bodine from Forrester, called *Outside In: The Power of Putting Customers at the Center of Your Business*, which provides an amazing foundation on CX. While the book is a must-read for CX professionals seeking to build foundational knowledge, it covers a lot of ground, from CX strategy to culture. Its focus on customer measurement and feedback is necessarily brief.

Given this, there is a need for a book to provide answers to the most important questions on building a world-class VoC program. This is what I am aiming to achieve here.

This book is written primarily for CX professionals in enterprise companies who are in charge of listening to customers (VoC). It is also relevant for anyone who is interested in CX or wants to learn more about how customer feedback can be used to drive business results. Entrepreneurs looking for a crash course on how to best listen to customers and use that feedback to improve their business will benefit from this book as well.

This book is organized into 40 lessons. My goal is to give you practical advice that you can implement now!

Most of the lessons are short, with some going into more detail than others. Be sure to check out (pun intended) the checklist at the end of each lesson as well. Each checklist contains four to eight items that distill the lesson into what you need to know and do right now to start or improve your customer listening program. There is also a space for you to take notes on what resonated with you the most in each lesson—or better yet, list the actions you're going to take now to start improving!

You can choose to read only the lessons or read only the checklists, though I highly recommend that you do both, as I'm sure you'll find hidden gems and additional recommendations throughout that stand out for your organization.

This book will guide you no matter where you are in your

VoC journey. If you plan to lead a new VoC program, you'll learn how to start it. If you've been collecting customer feedback for a year or so, you'll get strategies for ramping it up. If your VoC program is more mature, you'll find out how to make it ten times more effective.

My goal is for you to find answers to at least some of your burning questions, including those you didn't know to ask.

Let's dig right in.

SECTION ONE

WHAT YOU NEED TO KNOW BEFORE YOU START

LESSON #1

★ ★ ★ ★ ★

EVERYONE WANTS TO BE CUSTOMER-CENTRIC, BUT NO ONE KNOWS WHAT THAT MEANS.

Listen to any company in almost every industry, and you'll undoubtedly hear phrases like *customer-centric* and *customer-focused* touted as top priorities. But what does that exactly mean? When leaders of a company fail to explain or provide specific examples of what it really means to be customer-centric, employees often see these words as little more than corporate platitudes. I often get feedback from our clients' employees who say they don't know what it *means* to be customer-centric and certainly don't know how to practice it.

Here's the deal. Companies feel obligated to go on record as being customer-centric. It makes sense. Which company is going to publicly announce that they do *not* care about customers and what they have to say? But the reality is that becoming truly customer-centric is about more than developing vague marketing statements. The more important question is this: "As an organization, what can we do *today* to put the customer first?"

And to really make this really real, each employee at a customer-centric organization should ask themselves this question: "What *I* can do today to create a better customer experience for our customer?"

The reality is that becoming truly customer-centric is more than developing marketing statements—it is a fundamental shift in a company's mindset to focus on the customer.

The best way I know for companies to actually become more customer-centric is to consistently listen to the customer. Period. It starts and ends there. In fact, as the title of this book implies, I believe that the choice is simple—either listen to your customers or die. It sounds a bit dramatic, but it is true. Ask RadioShack, Blockbuster, BlackBerry, Kodak, and any other companies that were once on top and then stopped listening to their customers.

In my business, and throughout this book, I recommend accomplishing customer centricity by using an organization-wide, customer listening program called Voice of the Customer (VoC).

VoC gathers customer feedback during, or soon after, an experience. Then customer feedback is delivered to the people within the organization who are responsible for improving the experience and *immediately* resolving any issues identified by the customer. Resolving customer issues immediately increases the likelihood that you will retain customers and reduce churn. This is a marked departure from when all customer feedback lived in the market research department and was often confined to a handful of people within the organization. More on that in Lesson 8.

Here's the key point for now: when customer feedback reaches those who interact with customers every day (usually called the *front line* or *operators*), and they are empowered to act on this feedback and save potentially lost customers, a CX mindset is extended to the entire company. Your company begins to become customer-centric!

VoC also makes it easy for customers to be heard no matter how they choose to interact with your company. I refer to these interactions as *touchpoints* throughout the book. VoC tells you which touchpoints are going well (a hotel's spa, for example) and which are not (perhaps the hotel's in-house restaurant or front desk service). Much more to come on touchpoints later.

Here's some gold early in the book—if you remember only

what follows, you are already ahead of the game regarding customer listening. Regular customer listening enables your company to be more customer-centric by:

★ Immediately resolving individual customer problems as soon as possible before you lose that customer and/or they spread negative word of mouth (often through social media). Reducing customer churn and increasing the chances that a customer will provide a positive social review (or reducing the chances they will share a negative one) are two major business benefits of customer listening programs.

★ Understanding, at a strategic level, how customers feel about the various touchpoints, so you know where you are strong and where you need improvement.

★ Improving the touchpoints that aren't working, starting with the ones most likely to cost you customers or entice them to share negative feedback on social media.

CHECKLIST FOR BECOMING CUSTOMER-CENTRIC

☐ **When everyone in your organization can identify** how they individually are helping the company become closer to the customer, then you are a customer-centric organization. Before then, it's marketing.

☐ **Listening to your customer on a regular basis** and

acting on their feedback (i.e., VoC) to reduce churn makes customer centricity real. This will also change the culture of your organization like nothing else.

☐ **Remember that customer feedback drives real business results,** specifically reducing customer churn, increasing social review scores, and providing new sales leads that drive top-line revenue. Make sure your customer listening program delivers these outcomes.

☐ **Make sure customer feedback is available to your entire organization** (especially employees on the front line who are responsible for delivering a great customer experience), not just marketing or market research.

☐ **Gathering customer feedback is a journey, not a one-time event.** Make sure you are identifying key touchpoints that really matter to your customer, and continuously listen to their feedback.

NOTES

LESSON #2

★ ★ ★ ★ ★

CX MEASUREMENT IS HOT, BUT IT'S NOT WHAT YOU THINK IT IS.

As noted previously, the term *VoC* is frequently used to describe the measurement of the customer experience; so is the term *customer experience management* (CEM). A consulting firm mentioned in the introduction, Forrester, coined a third term: *customer feedback management* (CFM).

In this book, you'll see VoC more than any other term, though you can use each of these terms interchangeably. So, what is CX measurement or VoC? Let's start with what it is not.

As I mentioned in Lesson 1 and will dive into deeply in Lesson 8, VoC is *not* market research. Market research provides answers to a specific question and provides those answers in the aggregate. And in providing these answers, market researchers often wisely take a small sample of the overall population, which is less expensive and faster than surveying all customers. Market research methods are great for solving the right problem, and I am a big fan, but it's not VoC and it's not the optimal approach to customer experience management.

For example, consider a telecommunications company whose business model is signing up customers for a one-year contract for various wireless services. One month in, a customer feature disappears, such as transcription of voicemail to text; new customers may see the change as a bait and switch, while those close to renewal of their contract may think about switching to another carrier, and they begin to flood social media with complaints. Market researchers might not ever know about the problem, since they usually survey a sample of their customers and may do so only once a year, if at all. So a company with 100,000 customers might hear from 500 customers total and only if they happen to have scheduled a market research study during that time frame.

VoC, on the other hand, provides *daily* customer feedback that allows the organization to discover that the feature was a favorite in real time and that customers value it as part of their daily experience. VoC is about continuous, real-time feedback. In this example, VoC would reveal negative customer sentiment immediately, allowing the telecommunications company to course-correct. VoC allows customer issues to get identified and resolved before they require a separate study by market researchers!

Without a doubt, the job of market researchers is important; it's just very different than VoC. Plus, the findings from a typical market research study aren't typically shared across the entire organization, and there's no expectation of follow-up with individual customers providing the feedback. In fact, customers who provide feedback for market research are anonymous.

What's interesting is that, in some companies, the head of market research is also responsible for VoC! In Lesson 8, I discuss how this actually makes sense and how market researchers are using VoC to get answers to pressing questions in super-short time frames and tight budgets.

Okay, so CX measurement (VoC) is not market research. Then what is it? Simply put, it's the process of collecting and acting on customer feedback that was collected during or shortly after a recent experience. And customer feedback is usually identified, not anonymous.

HERE'S A QUICK GUIDE ON THE DIFFERENT TYPES OF FEEDBACK RANKED BY THEIR LEVEL OF CONNECTION TO VOC, FROM MOST TO LEAST:

Transactional surveys provide *solicited* customer feedback about their most recent experience (also referred to as CEM or CFM, as noted earlier). As the names imply, these surveys reach out to customers during or soon after an individual experience (e.g., visit to store, call to contact center, visit to website). These surveys are *not* anonymous, and customers often have an expectation that the company will follow up based on negative feedback provided. This is primarily the type of feedback I am referring to throughout most of this book.

Social reviews provide *unsolicited* customer feedback about a recent experience and are key to a comprehensive VoC program. Gathering feedback from social review sites like TripAdvisor, Yelp, and Google Reviews is an essential VoC task. This feedback is especially important in business-to-consumer (B2C) industries, such as hotels and restaurants. Similar to transactional surveys, customers often expect the company to respond, especially if the social review was negative.

Relationship surveys, as the name implies, help companies gauge the strength of their relationship with customers and are often used to get VoC off the ground. Relationship surveys are usually sent to *every* customer who's had an experience with the company in a given period—for example, in the past six months. Questions on a relationship survey will probe into overall customer feelings about a company based on a series of cumulative experiences, rather than a specific or recent experience. They also can include questions about customers' experience with competing brands and identify gaps compared to these competitors. Relationship surveys are a great way to start a

VoC program by getting a baseline on where you are today. These surveys will also help you ask the right questions for the touchpoints that really matter to your customers and are usually well worth the investment!

Market research surveys seek anonymously provided, solicited feedback, typically from a small sample of statistically relevant customers, on key strategic questions. For example, which advertising messages resonate best with a specific audience, or what is the optimal price for a new product? Market research surveys are usually one-off, meaning that once a company gathers the necessary data, they move on to their next study.

Focus groups are a popular way to gauge customer opinion, but they tend to have little or nothing to do with VoC. They are conducted with eight to ten people in a room with a one-way mirror. A moderator asks the group about something specific, such as whether they would consider using a new product, and the responses are recorded as a form of unstructured, qualitative feedback. Online focus groups are another way to gather qualitative feedback from customers. These are similar to in-person focus groups, except customers join an online forum to provide their opinions.

CHECKLIST FOR UNDERSTANDING CX MEASUREMENT (VOC)

☐ **Remember that there are many terms** that describe the activity of measuring the customer experience, including VoC, CEM, and CFM. These terms are all basically referring to the same thing: the continuous measurement of the customer experience either during or immediately after an experience and enabling the organization to follow up with that individual customer, who is usually identified and wants to receive a response to their feedback.

- [ ] **CX measurement (termed VoC in this book) is *not* the same as market research,** which is aimed at answering a specific strategic question, is anonymous, is often based on a small customer sample, and has a set beginning and end (i.e., it's not continuous).

- [ ] **There are two types of core CX measurement:** solicited feedback driven by surveys sent to customers soon after an experience, and unsolicited feedback driven by consumers providing social reviews of recent experiences on sites such as TripAdvisor, Yelp, and Google+.

- [ ] **When customers cite problems based on a recent customer experience** via either solicited or unsolicited channels, customers expect the company to follow up. For solicited surveys, the follow-up is usually a phone call or email to the customer. For unsolicited social reviews, the follow-up is usually first a public response on the social review site itself and second, if the customer gives permission and contact information, a direct dialogue.

- [ ] **A relationship survey is a great way to kick-start VoC.** These surveys gauge the strength of the relationship you have with customers. These are quick to get off the ground and yield valuable insights as to where you are right now with your customer experience.

NOTES

LESSON #3

★ ★ ★ ★ ★

VOC IS BECOMING THE SINGLE SOURCE OF TRUTH FOR ALL CUSTOMER FEEDBACK ON CX.

The best VoC programs are squarely focused on integrating all types of customer feedback related to the customer experience. The result is that VoC becomes the single source of truth for all experiential customer feedback. And a key part of making this happen is your VoC software platform. Every company that is serious about being customer-centric and listening to customers must invest in a VoC software platform that helps them collect customer feedback, quickly understand what it means, and act on it. It is an absolute must.

In Lesson 2, I introduced the primary types of VoC feedback—transactional surveys (solicited feedback) and social reviews (unsolicited feedback). Now I will expand on both of these and introduce a couple of additional types of feedback that are specific to understanding the customer experience: *verified* and *observed* feedback.

★ **Solicited:** The core of most VoC programs, solicited transactional surveys reach out to customers during or immediately after an experience. They are primarily distributed via email or text. No matter how the company solicits the customer feedback, it is something that companies directly request, therefore the term *solicited*. As introduced in Lesson 2, relationship surveys are also solicited and are often used as part of a comprehensive VoC program, although they are not transactional and focus on *all* your active customers rather than those who had a recent experience.

★ **Unsolicited:** Customers are increasingly volunteering feedback directly to the company or indirectly through social review sites. Unsolicited feedback is primarily thought of as social reviews but can also include calls to a company's contact center to complain about an issue or feedback through the "contact us" feature on a company-supplied app or website. All of these means are unsolicited, in that the company did not reach out directly asking for feedback from the customer. Out of all the unsolicited feedback channels, social reviews are the most powerful and need careful attention (see Lesson 29).

★ **Verified:** Verified feedback comes from experts, commonly called *mystery shoppers* or *quality assurance professionals*, who are hired to assess the experience that a company provides its customers. While this is not true "customer" feedback, it provides an important evaluation of the customer experience. Here's how this typically works. At a hotel, quality assurance (QA) professionals pretend to be a typical guest and have a checklist that reflects all the touchpoints a real guest might experience. For example, how fast was the check-in? Did the person at the front desk greet the guests by their name and smile? How long was the line? Was the bed made? Was the rug clean? Did the bathroom's soap dispenser contain soap? Did the remote control have that paper band on it that supposedly indicates it's clean? Answers to these questions provide a surrogate for the quality of the customer experience, because the QA professional is acting as a customer! Another type of verified feedback often used by a hotel might come from people within a company. These inspectors travel from company headquarters to each location to check on compliance with safety and brand standards. Specific standards might include anything from signage to uniforms to freezer temperatures. The goal is to create a consistent customer experience at every one of their locations. This is all "verified" feedback because it is provided by experts. RizePoint (www.rizepoint.com) is a PeopleMetrics partner and provides the best software in the quality assurance and brand compliance space. I highly recommend RizePoint if you are looking to include verified feedback within your VoC.

★ **Observed:** Your company might also consider a fourth type of feedback—observed. Some customers won't complain no matter how unhappy they are. It's only their behavior that gives away their true feelings. Consider a restaurant experience in which a customer doesn't say a word, but when the server collects the plates, a dish with no food eaten goes back to the kitchen untouched. Or consider a company that purchased a CRM software product and their salespeople rarely log on to use it. Or consider a coffee shop whose lines are so long that customers abandon the line and leave the store before purchasing. Analyzing and predicting consumer behavior (also called *Big Data*) also falls into this category. Collecting and organizing such observed feedback and behaviors requires integration with operational systems and your VoC software platform. It's often a heavy lift, but the benefits are well worth it.

For you to have a single source of truth around customer feedback data, you must implement a system of record, which is typically called a *VoC software platform*. The good news is that advanced VoC software platforms can bring all types of customer feedback together under one roof, providing a single, comprehensive source of truth about an organization's true, start-to-finish customer experience! This provides unprecedented opportunities to improve the customer experience. You are living in the right time to deliver exceptional customer experiences!

CHECKLIST FOR GETTING TO THE TRUTH

☐ **Make sure you consider all the sources of feedback** on the customer experience. And there are many! Solicited, unsolicited, verified, and observed are the primary types.

☐ **Be aware of all types of customer feedback,** but you need to start somewhere to begin your journey to find your single source of truth. This is often solicited transactional survey feedback via a key touchpoint that matters to your customers. A relationship survey is another great way to start your VoC.

☐ **Once you have solicited feedback humming,** integrate key unsolicited feedback channels, especially social reviews, if they're appropriate for your industry. There is incredible power in viewing solicited and unsolicited feedback together in one dashboard or report.

☐ **Verified feedback and observed feedback are not obvious** but can bring a real rigor to your VoC program or take it to the next level.

☐ **Make sure your VoC software platform is capable of combining** these different types of CX feedback in a way that makes sense and is accessible to people in your organization.

☐ **Mine your VoC software platform to get to the truth.** Exciting machine learning options are becoming available to help in this regard and are explained in Lesson 38.

NOTES

LESSON #4

★ ★ ★ ★ ★

TEXT ANALYTICS IS MORE THAN A VOC FEATURE; IT'S AN ABSOLUTE MUST-HAVE.

The true "voice" of your customer is the unique words they share with you each time you ask them "why" or "please tell me more about that" in your survey. There is gold in each comment that customers share with you. The question is this: how do you best mine for that gold? Enter text analytics.

But first, let's take a step back. No matter how you are listening to customers (solicited, unsolicited, verified, observed), the data you will ultimately collect will be one of two types: structured or unstructured.

STRUCTURED FEEDBACK

Structured customer feedback is the most common, the easiest to deal with, and super important in spite of this lesson's title. Let's consider an example. A typical question in your transactional (solicited) survey might be, "How satisfied were you with your most recent experience at Hotel ABC on a scale of 1 to 5, with 5 being very satisfied and 1 being very dissatisfied?" When customers provide their answer to this question, it comes in the form of a number—in this case, a 5 would indicate *very satisfied* with the most recent visit to the hotel, a 1 would indicate *very dissatisfied*, and so on. Almost any VoC software platform can easily analyze these data and create graphs to aggregate and compare the responses: Maybe 30% of respondents were very satisfied, 35% very dissatisfied, and so forth. For example, consider this graph, which is easily rendered based on structured responses.

NPS Segments

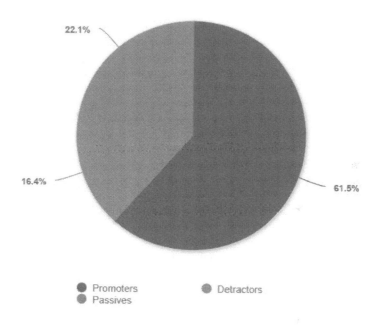

22.1%

16.4%

61.5%

● Promoters ● Detractors
● Passives

What's not easy is unstructured customer feedback that often follows a structured question.

UNSTRUCTURED FEEDBACK

Unstructured feedback is key to understanding why those satisfaction levels are what they are. Continuing with our earlier example, the next question in the survey might be "Please tell us why you feel that way." This is prompting the customer to type in open-ended (unstructured) comments to explain their level of satisfaction with the experience. A customer might type in something like "The front desk took too long to check in," "The room was dirty," or "The people staying in the room next to me were loud and I didn't get any sleep."

And these unstructured comments are not just for solicited, transactional surveys. Unstructured customer feedback is key to unsolicited feedback as well, especially social reviews. Visitors to review sites like TripAdvisor can write entire paragraphs of open-ended feedback on their recent experience. Unstructured feedback is incredibly valuable because it indicates *why* people feel the way they do. Without it, CX professionals would be lost. How would they know what to do to fix problems without context?

A UNIFYING FRAMEWORK

I have introduced a lot of terms regarding types of feedback. The ones you need to know as a CX professional are solicited, unsolicited, structured, and unstructured. The following is a unifying framework that gives examples that I hope will make this clear.

	Solicited	Unsolicited
Structured	Surveys	Social Reviews
Unstructured	Open Ends (Text Analytics)	Call Center Notes Web Forums Social Chatter

MAKING SENSE OF UNSTRUCTURED FEEDBACK

The question then becomes this: how do we make sense out of these unstructured comments from customers? Unlike structured data, which are easy to display graphically or in tables, each piece of unstructured data is different—unique to each customer who took the time to provide it.

There are two options to handle unstructured feedback: humans or machines.

Humans are the most expensive method to make sense of unstructured comments—often prohibitively so, because not only are they expensive knowledge workers but also the effort doesn't scale. An approach to unstructured data analysis made popular with market researchers is called *open-ended coding.* Here's how it works.

A person is tasked with reviewing a small sample (one hundred is common) of open-ended customer comments and the goal is to identify major "themes" from these comments. They create what is called a "codebook" that contains a handful of major themes (usually five to ten). Then usually another person reviews the remainder of the open ends, one by one, and assigns one of the major themes to each comment. We are talking about thousands of comments in some circumstances and days or weeks of work. The result is that unstructured comments become structured! Then market researchers create a report that quantifies these comments—such as 43% of people mentioned Wi-Fi as a problem, 16% mentioned the spa as an issue, and so on.

The human approach is virtually impossible to scale. For PeopleMetrics' larger clients, we send out more than 20,000 surveys a week, which results in thousands of open-ended responses. In a given day, even the best human coders might be able to handle a few hundred comments.

Machines (text analytics), on the other hand, can scale infinitely. All sophisticated VoC software platforms will have a text analytics module available. Let's dig into the value that text analytics provides.

Using a computer algorithm that identifies common themes or topics by scanning and grouping customer comments, text analytics provides an unprecedented ability to make sense and take action on large volumes of unstructured customer feedback. Here's how it works. *Wi-Fi* could be a topic, but some customers might call it *wireless internet*. Others might say only *internet* or *speed of internet* or *web access*. After a little tuning by a human, the machine quickly learns to identify all those terms as Wi-Fi. The next step is that the machine is trained to understand customer sentiment for each comment. One customer might say, "I love this hotel because the wifi is so fast." Another customer's comment could be, "wifi, there was nothing fast about it, so frustrating." The machine then assigns a sentiment score for each comment related to given topics, usually ranging from −1 to +1.

Then text analytics organizes all topics in a visual display, often in the form of a word cloud. If you've seen one, you already know that the size of each word reflects how often the topic is mentioned. Its color indicates the sentiment: red usually indicates negative, green for positive, and yellow for neutral. The image here shows an example from a retail bank.

Text analytics can quickly identify trends in real time and at scale. This allows you to identify and get in front of major problems immediately! By contrast, human coders might take weeks to notice that, say, the bank's pricing is an issue, as in the earlier example.

Using a machine also guarantees *consistency* of your classifications over time. There are times when the coding approach changes as the focus of the business changes. Perhaps a hotel lobby had a major renovation and was renamed "The Lounge." The hotel wants to know if customers' sentiment toward The Lounge improved after the renovations. Previously, the coders did not consider the lobby as a topic when they were coding open ends. If this happens, a decision has to be made about recoding historical information: is it worth having employees spend weeks rereading numerous open-ended comments? For machines, though, an almost unlimited number of open-ended comments can be reprocessed instantaneously, guaranteeing that the hotel can gauge if their investment in The Lounge was worth the cost. While text analytics can't match the accuracy of human coders (at least right now)—as high as 95% accurate for humans, compared with 80% to 85% for text analytics—with volume and time, text-analytics programs *learn*.

Indeed, as more people examine text analytics output, it becomes more accurate. When people spot contradictions (for example, maybe respondents reported super-fast Wi-Fi by saying, "This Wi-Fi was killing it," but the machine rated the sentiment as negative) and correct them, they are training the machine to do better the next time.

Human coders, on the other hand, are more likely to become *less* accurate with higher volume and time. What's more, human coding is a siloed activity, usually involving one person working from a codebook that someone else— probably within their department—created. By nature, the process can't benefit from the genius of a group and is unlikely to produce new insights. Faced with a long comment, a human typically skims it for words they're *used* to seeing; they're not looking for anything new. The machine, which neither bores nor tires, can identify both familiar words and emerging outliers.

Finally, human coders can't even begin to compete with

text analytics in speed and cost. Although it costs more up front to set up text analytics—maybe $10,000 to $20,000—the cost per comment when it's up and running is minimal. Costs will not continue to build with volume, while you might pay humans a dollar or two per comment indefinitely.

Given that response rates are dropping for longer surveys, you need to get more out of fewer questions, including one or maybe two open-ended questions at the most. Plus, with the continuing growth of social media, you can expect to receive more unstructured feedback in the form of social reviews. This is why I am saying that text analytics is not a feature of VoC; it *is* VoC. It's the only way you can stay on top of key trends in a cost-efficient manner at scale.

And if you're still concerned about the difference in accuracy between open-ended coding and text analytics, let it go! Consider the trade-off between greater accuracy on every comment and the ability to spot key trends in real time that will help you improve CX!

In reality, if you don't have a quick, accurate, and affordable way to process your unstructured customer feedback, collecting it in the first place is a pointless exercise. Text analytics represents the present and future; without it, you are not getting all you can out of your VoC program.

	TA	OE
ACCURACY PER COMMENT	80%–85%	95%+
PURPOSE	Identify trends at scale	Create a report/results from qualitative data
SPEED	Real time	Long time
COST	Cheap	Expensive
CONSISTENCY	Very consistent	Varies (prone to human bias)
ORIGIN	Natural Language Processing	Market Research
SOCIAL	Crowdsource (collaborative, becomes better over time, potential for higher validity)	Siloed (limited to skills of the coder, potential bias)
SCALE	Unlimited (infinity!)	Limited (hundreds per day per coder)

CHECKLIST FOR TEXT ANALYTICS MASTERY

☐ **Get your text analytics mindset right**—text analytics is not the same as open-ended coding. It is the only way for you to spot key CX trends in real time with high volumes of unstructured data, and it can pay for the entire VoC program investment many times over, if done right. Appreciate text analytics for what it is; do not focus on what it is not.

☐ **If you are considering a new VoC software platform**, make sure you ask the providers if their text analytics module is "native" (i.e., developed in-house). This is important because if it is not native text analytics, it means the provider is using third-party software. The result could result in great pain if you require custom features or changes to how text analytics works for your organization.

☐ **Make sure you train text analytics** so it understands your business. Text analytics is powerful, but it is not magic. It needs help in terms of training it to understand the language your customers are using. A good partner or internal expert can help train text analytics so it performs the way you expect.

☐ **Expect good but not perfect accuracy.** Human coders can achieve 95% accuracy or higher, while a well-trained text analytics package can hit 85% or so.

☐ **Don't stop training!** You would not work out once at a gym and expect results to last forever. Similarly, you need to revisit your training approach to text analytics every so often to make sure it is keeping up with current customer commentary.

NOTES

LESSON #5

★ ★ ★ ★ ★

YOU'VE GOT TO KNOW AND USE NPS, EVEN IF YOU DON'T LIKE IT.

An important metric in any successful VoC program is NPS, or Net Promoter Score. You should know a lot about NPS before you begin VoC. This is why this lesson is so early in the book.

NPS is well known across industries, in companies of all sizes, and throughout executive boardrooms. In fact, NPS is regularly reported in some quarterly results, and it has become the de facto standard for how well companies are doing with their customers.

The concept of NPS was created by Fred Reichheld, the author of *The Ultimate Question: Driving Good Profits and True Growth*. NPS has become so popular, and so widely used, that it truly has become the ultimate question in the VoC world. It's important to keep in mind that NPS is a straightforward question that measures your *overall relationship* with your customer based on the bundle of experiences they have had with you *over time*.

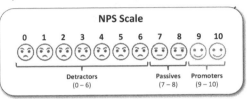

Thinking about your overall relationship with (company), how likely are you to recommend them to family, friends, and/or colleagues?

Detractors (0 thru 6)	Passives (7 or 8)	Promoters (9 or 10)
• Unhappy customers • Account for 80%+ of negative word-of-mouth[1] • Most likely to defect or choose a competitor when given the option	• Satisfied but by no means wowed by the services they are receiving • Less likely to give a referral and are likely to be unenthusiastic when they do • Not necessarily looking to defect but may do so if presented with other options	• Most exuberant customers • Singing high praises to friends and colleagues • Account for 80%+ of referrals[1] • Most likely to remain customers or choose you over the competition

1. Bain & Company: Measuring Your Net Promoter Score

Why is NPS so powerful? For one, it's simple to calculate and understand. NPS is a single question that asks the customer, "How likely are you to recommend (company) to a friend, colleague, or family member, on a scale of 0 to 10?" Zero means that the customer is very unlikely to recommend the company, whereas a 10 means that their recommendation is very likely.

Customers who answer with a number from 0 to 6—called *detractors*—are subtracted from the *promoters*, or those who answer with a 9 or 10. For example, if eight out of ten customers answered with a 9 or 10, then 80% of your customers are promoters. If 5% answered with a 0 to 6, they are unlikely to recommend your company, and that 5% would be subtracted from your promoter total of 80. Your NPS is 75.

Calculating the NPS Score	Reasoning

NPS = Promoters - Detractors
 	
Example:
    Promoters = 80% of customers
    Passives = 15% of customers
    Detractors = 5% of customers
        NPS = 80 - 5 = 75
 	
Scores range from **-100** (100% Detractors, 0% Passives, 0% Promoters) to **100** (0% Detractors, 0% Passives, 100% Promoters)
	Promoters are most likely to be advocates and remain loyal to the brand
	
	Detractors are most likely to spread negative word of mouth and defect
	
	Passives are neither likely to be advocates nor to provide negative word of mouth. They are also generally not actively looking defect but are not loyal to the brand. They have no positive or negative impact on the calculation, however a large population of Passives will restrict the range of the Net Promoter Score

Customers who answer with a 7 or 8 are categorized as *passives*. Passives don't figure into the NPS calculation but are important to consider as well.

NPS allows you to draw insights by comparing promoters, passives, and detractors. Are promoters more likely to buy your new product or expand their relationship with you? What do you need to do to move a customer from being a detractor to a promoter? NPS allows you to dig into these questions and many more.

NPS is also easy to understand, with the score represented as a single number falling anywhere between –100 and +100. Because that simple score grabs the attention of executives, NPS will build VoC credibility and focus within the organization. And because it's a common metric across industries, it also provides you with the opportunity to benchmark your NPS compared to other companies in your industry or other industries.

WHAT'S A GOOD NPS?

I often get asked what is considered a "good" NPS. Well, a "bad" NPS is certainly anything in the negative territory. In other words, if you have more detractors than promoters, you have a big problem. A good NPS is trickier and requires benchmarks to compare yourself to other firms.

Temkin Group (www.temkingroup.com) does an annual study on the customer experience across many different industries and reports on NPS. I consider their study to be the gold standard in NPS benchmarks, and I highly recommend you subscribe to their excellent research. Temkin Group is also a great resource if your team needs training on CX, leadership coaching, journey mapping, or other consulting services related to CX.

The included table shows the results from a recent Temkin Group benchmark study. You can see that any NPS score above 60 is considered world class, with companies such as USAA and Apple as examples. An NPS of 40-59 is still considered very strong, and you should be excited to hit this range. You would be in the same company as customer-focused companies such as Amazon and Hilton. When you get below 40, then there are some issues, mainly around the fact that many of your customers are passives and could be vulnerable to turning into detractors in the future. Geico and Home Depot are examples of companies in the 25-40 NPS range. An NPS below 25 is when you have real problems. This is when you have many more passives and detractors than promoters. We are talking about companies like Spirit Airlines and Motel 6. Finally, as I mentioned earlier, a negative NPS is unacceptable. This means a majority of your customers are detractors, and you need a major overhaul. Cable TV providers are a classic example of companies with negative NPS.

NPS = 60+	A world class score, the majority of customers are enthusiastic and loyal supporters of your brand, with few Detractors. Generally seen for premium brands that offer industry leading services and customer experience
	Companies: USAA (63), Apple (60)
NPS = 40 thru 59	A strong score with opportunity for improvement based the mix of Passives and Detractors. At the upper end of the scale are customer-centric brands generally offering high end services. The lower end of the scale represents companies with a strong focus on customer experience, though offer more generally commoditized services. <ul><li>High level of Detractors may imply a dislocation the quality of services provided within a region or demographic group</li><li>High level of Passives may imply a need to make systemic improvements to the customer experience to help differentiate from the competition</li></ul>
	Companies: Amazon (59), Hilton (45)
NPS = 25 thru 39	A weaker score with a substantial portion of customers generally being Passives. Generally associated with "every day" brands.
	Companies: GEICO (37), Home Depot (33)
NPS = 0 thru 24	A very weak score with a substantial portion of customers being Passives or Detractors. This range is generally seen for industries that provide "basic" products & services, industries associated with negative experiences, or industries with partial or local monopolies.
	Companies: Spirit Airlines (18), Motel 6 (4)
Negative NPS	A poor score with the majority of customers being detractors. Companies with a poor public perception that are associated with a generally unpleasant customer experience.
	Companies: Time Warner Cable (-3), Comcast TV Services (-5)

Source: Temkin Group Q3 2016 Consumer Benchmark Survey

AN ALTERNATIVE TO NPS

NPS is not the only game in town. An alternative to NPS is typically an *index of key questions that also aims to measure the strength of the overall relationship companies have with their customers*. With an index, companies combine three or more items and create their own version of NPS.

Some of PeopleMetrics' clients use a *customer loyalty index* (CLI) as an alternative to NPS. The CLI consists of three items: 1) how likely customers are to recommend (essentially NPS), 2) how satisfied customers are overall, and 3) how likely customers are to return or buy again. The scale on these questions is usually a 5-point scale, with 5 being the most positive response. Customers who answer positively (i.e., those who indicate a 4 or 5) to *all three* questions are considered "loyal" customers. Those who essentially disagree with any of those three items are considered not loyal. This is another method to get a single score; in this case, the score is the percentage of customers considered loyal. The range for CLI is 0% to 100%.

CLI Components
(Scale 1-5)

SATISFACTION	ADVOCACY	RETENTION
Overall, how satisfied were you with your most recent visit to (company)?	How likely would you be to recommend (company), to a friend or colleague?	Where you to have a choice, how likely would you be to choose (company), again?

Loyalty Segments

Customer Advocate	"5" on satisfaction, advocacy, and retention questions
Loyal Customer	"4 or 5" on satisfaction, advocacy, and retention questions (but at least one "4")
On-the-Fence Customer	"3, 4, or 5" on satisfaction, advocacy, and retention questions (but at least one "3")
Hostile Customer	At least one "2" on satisfaction, advocacy, and retention questions

Calculating CLI

Customer Loyalty Index = % Customer Advocates i.e. Rating 5's for all 3 components of Loyalty

Some of our clients segment their customers even further based on CLI. In the diagram shown, customers are segmented in one of four groups: customer advocate, loyal customer, on-the-fence customer, or hostile customer. In this example, all customers other than customer advocates are not considered truly *secure*.

As you can see, the equations for identifying segments based on CLI are more complex, customized, and precise than NPS. However, you do get a better sense of the degree to which each customer is loyal to you with CLI. A hostile customer is often very different than an on-the-fence customer. NPS blends the hostile and on-the-fence groups into detractors. There are big differences between a customer who is outraged and one who is on the fence. Similarly, the passives in NPS basically consist of a blend of on-the-fence and loyal customers in the CLI framework. There are key differences between these customer groups as well.

USING NPS DESPITE ITS FLAWS

The advantage of NPS over an index like CLI is clear: the simplicity of NPS makes it easier for executives to understand and allows easy dissemination across the organization. However, NPS is not a flawless metric. It can provide excellent insight into the overall relationship you have with your customers, but it falls short in measuring how well the most recent experience went. Used as the only metric in transactional VoC surveys, valuable customer experience feedback may fall through the cracks.

For example, perhaps during a visit to a customer's favorite restaurant, everyone in their party got sick, the waiter was rude, or the service was unusually slow. When this customer is presented with the ultimate question (i.e., NPS), they may recommend the restaurant because it's their favorite based on many positive past experiences—but relying on NPS alone may not reveal the most recent issue. Again, NPS provides good insight into the overall customer *relationship* but is not the best measure of the most recent customer *experience*.

NPS also suffers from a user feedback experience perspective. Customers today prefer to complete surveys quickly and conveniently on their mobile devices, but NPS surveys can have problems displaying the 10-point scale within the small-screen real estate of some mobile devices. As a result, the response rate of the survey may be negatively impacted. Similarly, NPS presents limitations during telephone surveys—especially when the telephone survey uses an *interactive voice response*, or IVR. When the IVR asks the customer questions after a telephone conversation with the contact center, the computer must read the question *and* instruct the customer on using the scale. It takes a long time to read off the NPS question and the 10-point scale that follows.

Perhaps the biggest flaw in NPS is that it's a lagging metric. It asks the customer about their cumulative, overall opinion of the company. This feeling builds throughout the customer's *past* experiences but does not always indicate the customer's *future* actions and intentions.

However, rather than going to war against NPS (which plenty of people like to do; do a web search on it sometime), simply keep its limitations in mind.

NPS is most valuable when leveraged alongside other metrics. In a relationship survey, you should use NPS or CLI. These are both excellent measures of the overall relationship you have with your customers.

I completely understand that sometimes your bandwidth or budget will not be enough for a full relationship survey, but you still need to report on NPS. This is when NPS should be used with a transactional VoC survey with an additional question immediately following that is used to determine specifics about the most recent customer experience. This way, you get to regularly report on NPS to executives and have the data you need to respond to recent customer experiences.

Customer Loyalty Index	Net Promoter Score
Advantages: • Captures multiple dimensions of loyalty in one composite score • Greater sensitivity to possible transactional as well as systemic issues • Shown to be correlated with business performance across industries and companies **Disadvantages:** • Not always the industry standard • Its relative complexity makes it more difficult to interpret and explain to key stakeholders	**Advantages:** • Simple and easy to assimilate at all levels in the organization • Shown to be correlated with future revenue growth across several industries • Often the industry-standard calculation **Disadvantages:** • Single-item outcome score has been shown to be less reliable than a composite measure • NPS measures just one element of customer engagement: Advocacy

CHECKLIST FOR MASTERING NPS FUNDAMENTALS

☐ **First, understand what NPS is best for—measuring the overall relationship** you have with your customers. It is *not* a measure of the most recent customer experience.

☐ **Always use NPS or an alternative like the Customer Loyalty Index (CLI)** in a relationship survey where your objective is to understand how strong your overall bond is with your customers.

☐ **Do not solely rely on NPS to measure CX in a transactional survey;** include another measure to get at how well the most recent customer experience went (see more in Lesson 28).

☐ **Know what your NPS score means.** A negative NPS score means you have more detractors than promoters...and things need to change, quick! An NPS score above 60 will put you in the same company as the best companies in the world. Most likely, you will be between these extremes.

☐ **Be aware that NPS has flaws.** Besides not being a great measure of the most recent customer experience, it is a lagging measure, it is not the most customer-friendly metric for those on mobile devices with smaller screens or answering using IVR, and it's not as comprehensive as more robust indices like CLI.

☐ **Finally, even if you don't like NPS, use it anyway.** In the grand scheme of things, it's a solid measure of your overall relationship with customers. It's super easy to understand, and executives in your company will probably expect to see it. It's simply not worth fighting NPS.

NOTES

LESSON #6

★ ★ ★ ★ ★

YOU HAVE TO USE NPS, BUT YOU SHOULD ALSO INCLUDE OTHER MEASURES OF CX IN A TRANSACTIONAL VOC SURVEY.

As mentioned in the previous lesson, NPS is important to include in your VoC, but if you're running a transactional VoC survey, you need other ways to measure the most recent customer experience, along with NPS.

There are a few ways you can do this. You can simply ask how satisfied the customer was with their last experience. This question can be made more contextual by adding specific dates for their last experience: "During your visit to Hotel X on July 28 through July 30, how satisfied were you with the experience?"

Another approach is to focus on customer effort. You

can ask, "How much effort did you exert to solve your issue during your call on January 12?" The more effort a customer expends on resolving their issue, the more negative the customer experience. Effort is best used with a contact center touchpoint where customers typically are calling to resolve an issue. When they call a contact center, the customer expects the issue to be solved quickly so they can move on with their day. The idea is to deliver a customer experience with as little friction (i.e., customer effort) as possible.

A third option is simply to ask about their overall experience during their most recent visit. You can use a scale from delighted to disappointed.

If you want to measure the overall customer relationship in a transactional VoC survey, pick *either* NPS *or* a retention question, but you do not have to use both (unless you are creating an index; see Lesson 5). Customers who say they are likely to recommend the business will most likely return. Asking both questions can be redundant, especially if your goal is to make the survey as short as possible.

On the other hand, you *must* combine NPS with an individual measure of the customer experience in a transactional VoC survey. If you ignore customer issues from recent customer experiences, eventually your NPS will take a nosedive.

Let's say, for example, that a customer shops on Amazon frequently, and they've always received their products on time. Then one day, they order their son's birthday gift, and it arrives late, *after* his birthday.

Chances are good that this customer will still be a promoter when they're asked if they would recommend Amazon; at this point, if Amazon asks only the NPS question, they'll likely not know about the customer's single bad experience and won't take appropriate action. If the same customer uses Amazon again for their daughter's birthday gift and the package is once again late, Amazon's relationship with that customer is likely over—and what's worse is that Amazon may have no idea *why*. The company already had an opportunity to find out about the problem and fix it in their first survey, but the survey's design did not give them the answers they needed to prevent churn.

This is why it's important for transactional VoC surveys to measure the most recent customer experience. Back to the analogy that I introduced in the beginning of the book: Imagine customer experience as a bank account. Every negative experience is a withdrawal. The only time you will know the account is at zero is when you try to make a withdrawal and it's declined. You need to know continuously when withdrawals are being made so that you can *prevent* the customer experiential account from hitting zero and leaving you. Make sure that you catch each withdrawal and then redeposit goodwill by following up with the customer and making things right.

CHECKLIST FOR USING NPS IN TRANSACTIONAL VOC SURVEYS

☐ **If you need to report NPS to executives on a regular basis,** include it as your first question in your transactional VoC survey. Make sure it's included directly in your email invitation (see Lesson 27).

☐ **NPS will not be enough in your transactional VoC survey,** though; you must include another question that measures the most recent customer experience. You can use customer satisfaction, customer effort (great for the contact center touchpoint), or overall customer experience.

☐ **Make sure whatever question you use** to measure the most recent customer experience immediately follows NPS.

☐ **Your open-ended question should focus on your CX question,** *not* your NPS question. You want to get clarity over what you can do *now* to fix the most recent experience if there was an issue. And too many open-ended questions fatigue customers, so don't ask an open-ended question after both NPS and your recent CX question.

☐ **Improving NPS is about constantly following up** and fixing individual customer problems (this is a continuous process), then picking big systemic issues that are causing many customer problems and fixing these. This is the formula; there are no shortcuts.

NOTES

LESSON #7

★ ★ ★ ★ ★

CX IS *NOT* THE SAME AS *CUSTOMER SERVICE.* KNOW THE DIFFERENCE.

Customer service (CS) is often critical for delivering a great customer experience (CX). But CS is *not* the same as CX.

These terms are often used interchangeably, but they're not synonymous. It's key to remember that customer service is *part* of the overall customer experience, not the entire customer experience.

Let's first define customer experience and customer service. I define CX as the sum of all experiences, interactions, or touchpoints a customer has with a company. I define CS as employees at a company helping solve a customer's need in some way, usually but not always around a problem or a question. It is vital to understand the difference as you implement VoC.

CX is holistic. CX covers a wide number of touchpoints. Some of them are CS oriented, some are not. This concept is easiest to understand with an example. Let's take an example of getting broadband internet services installed at your home. Key touchpoints might include:

★ Going onto a company's website to check out pricing (*not* CS)
★ Calling their 800 number to ask questions (CS)
★ Going back to the website to purchase (*not* CS)
★ Having a technician come to your home for installation (CS)
★ Calling billing to ask questions about your first bill (CS)
★ Experiencing the service by watching videos on YouTube, downloading music, etc. (*not* CS)
★ Calling the company because your internet service is down (CS)
★ Going to the company's website to upgrade your service to include telephone services (*not* CS)

Doing this type of exercise in your business is extremely valuable. At PeopleMetrics, we call this *touchpoint mapping*, and there is a lesson dedicated to this (see Lesson 18). For now, let's remember that when you map out your touchpoints, note which ones are CS oriented and which ones are not but are still an important part of the customer experience. I bet you will find that many touchpoints that are key to the overall customer experience have nothing to do with customer service. A complete VoC program includes all touchpoints, including those that are product or digitally oriented.

One more word on this topic: You will sound much more informed if you are distinguishing between customer service and customer experience in your everyday communication. Make sure you talk about CS as vital to creating a great CX, but understand there is much more to it. Doing so will help both your company and your career!

CHECKLIST FOR NOT CONFUSING CS WITH CX

☐ **Remember the definitions of these terms**—CX is about all the interactions your customer has with your company, including digital, product, and service. CS is squarely focused on employees solving a customer problem, delivering a service, or answering a question.

☐ **Appreciate that CS is critical** to delivering a great CX, but it's not the same as CX.

☐ **If you are having a hard time making this distinction real**, try a touchpoint map where you list all the interactions or touchpoints your customers have with your company. Make sure you include digital and product-related touchpoints in your map. Then label each touchpoint as *CS* or *not CS*. You can refine this analysis by identifying touchpoints that are digital and product oriented.

☐ **When you are creating your VoC,** make sure that it is not a VoC on CS program only, and that you include non-CS touchpoints that are important to the overall customer experience. Start with your digital and product experiences.

☐ **When you are talking to others** within your company about CX, make sure you are clear that you are differentiating CX and CS.

NOTES

LESSON #8

★ ★ ★ ★ ★

VOC IS NOT THE SAME AS MARKET RESEARCH, BUT THEY'RE CONVERGING.

Market research is my background; I have my PhD in Marketing Science, and I originally started PeopleMetrics as a market research firm.

Years later, I sold half of the company—the market research division—to focus on CX and VoC. I didn't sell because of a lack of interest in market research, but because I recognized the crucial differences between market research and VoC. And I simply felt these two worlds were so different that if I wanted to do great work, I needed to concentrate on one of them.

Market research was developed a century ago to measure the effectiveness of advertisements and products. Today it's used in similar ways—to figure out competitive positioning, to determine the optimal price for new products, and to decide on the most effective advertising strategies (to name a few).

However, market research and VoC are not the same. In fact, certain principles that are key to market research hold back VoC and the value that companies get out of VoC. Let me explain.

As mentioned in Lesson 2, market researchers usually reach out to a small sample of customers for feedback on a wide variety of strategic topics and focus on aggregate results and trends. On the other hand, VoC typically includes a software platform that both gathers customer feedback on recent experiences and enables companies *to act on individual customer feedback*. As market researchers, we may ask you what you think of a new logo, a new advertising message, or how our client stacks up to their competition, but we will not share specific feedback from any individual respondent. The reason is that market researchers operate under an oath of respondent anonymity. Market researchers are also generally focused on getting an answer to a specific strategic question, which results in studies that have a distinct beginning and end.

With VoC, there is a dialogue between the customer and the business. The customer provides feedback about a recent experience—for instance, a bad meal at a favorite restaurant—and the business can follow up with that customer, ask additional questions, and try to resolve the situation. With market research, communication is one-way—we ask customers what they think about a certain issue, and outside of perhaps compensating the customer for their time, there is no communication back to that customer.

THE EVOLUTION OF FEEDBACK

When I first started in this business, if I told clients that we were going to survey all of their customers (rather than a small sample) and allow them to contact individual customers about their responses, they would have thought I was crazy. At that point, anything that might threaten respondent confidentiality and anonymity was not considered. Today, most customers *want* a business to follow up with them after providing feedback on a recent experience, especially if their feedback was negative.

So, what changed? The answer to that, I believe, is the emergence of Facebook, Twitter, Yelp, and people sharing what they ate for lunch on Instagram. These days, customers love to share their experiences with their friends and, oftentimes, the world. For CX leaders, the notion that customers can complain online instantly and have a wide audience should be front and center. They can even upload videos of their experiences—like when the Comcast technician fell asleep on the job (and the customer's couch).

Building on the viral aspect of customer feedback, VoC helps companies manage and at times avoid embarrassing social reviews. Customers regularly give permission for businesses to contact them after they complete surveys, and businesses have the opportunity to respond when customers share negative experiences. And if they do not reach out, a negative social review is likely right around the corner. In fact, at PeopleMetrics, 99% of customers we survey give permission for the company to follow up based on their survey feedback. The tide has completely changed from just a few years ago.

PRACTICAL DIFFERENCES

The important point here is that companies can use VoC to start a dialogue with all customers who have had a recent experience. While there are often rules in VoC so that customers are not over-surveyed, basically everyone has a voice. So all customers have an opportunity to provide feedback about their experience, rather than those in a sample population that market researchers usually reach.

Incentives are another key point of difference. Most of the time, incentives are required to get someone to complete a market research survey—why else would anyone take up to an hour out of their day to answer research questions? Market research surveys are often long, complicated, and almost impossible to do on mobile devices. Incentives are rarely used in VoC because surveys are usually brief, and if incentives are used, it's normally in the form of a sweepstakes (more on incentives in Lesson 28).

Market research is also limited to a snapshot of a time period. Businesses want specific information, so they ask a bunch of people and wait weeks to learn their customers' answers, and once the results are in, the process ends. VoC is in real time, continuous, and never-ending. While VoC has a strategic component, it's mostly operational. And the people who actually face customers receive feedback directly.

MERGING THE BEST OF BOTH WORLDS

Somewhat surprisingly, VoC and market research are coming together. The reason? VoC has become the source of truth (see Lesson 3) for customer feedback due to its continuous flow of real-time feedback from every customer (not just a sample of customers). Market researchers like this continuous access to customer feedback. Plus, the strategic angle of market research questions never goes away, and market research budgets are being tightened. The solution? Market research questions are showing up in VoC programs for a limited period of time and then "swapped out" for new questions when appropriate.

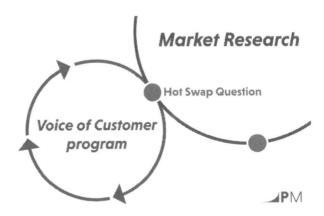

For example, we may ask customers in a transactional VoC survey, "What logo color do you like the best?" until we have 200-400 responses to this market research question. In this way, VoC is able to provide incredible value by delivering fast answers more affordably than if a separate market research study were commissioned.

Combining market research questions with VoC efficiency gives you an instant advantage. Rather than spending $100,000 for one market research study, organizations can save that budget for complex market research efforts that require experts, like a discrete choice modeling study to determine optimal price points for a new product.

As a CX leader, you can be a hero at your company if you work with your market research team to identify their most important questions and then work these questions into your VoC survey, so that your company gets quick feedback at a reasonable price. They will love it (and you) when they get fast answers to key questions that save their budgets.

	MR	VOC
COMMUNICATION WITH CUSTOMER	One-way	Two-way (encouraging dialogue)
ANALYSIS	Aggregate	Individual and aggregate
AUDIENCE	Sample of customers	Census
ACCESS TO RESULTS	MR team and product sponsor	Front line and everyone else
LENGTH OF SURVEY	Long	Short/brief
SPEED TO RESULTS	Weeks/months	Real time
INCENTIVES	Usually required	Limited/optional
TIMING	Point in time	Continuous
PURPOSE	Strategic	Strategic and operational
PARTICIPANT IDENTITY	Anonymous	Identified

CHECKLIST FOR CONVERGING VOC AND MARKET RESEARCH

☐ **Make sure you have a solid transactional VoC survey** up and running before you think about adding market research questions—it requires you to have a consistent stream of customer feedback flowing.

☐ **Develop a good relationship with your market research colleagues** and understand their needs.

☐ **Make sure your VoC software platform is capable of swapping** market research questions on a periodic basis and reporting results in the same software platform as your VoC results.

☐ **Create an ROI analysis** on the dollars you are saving on ad hoc market research studies through your VoC program.

☐ **Make sure you are able to provide** your market research colleagues with access to your VoC software platform. They can get the results they need and provide an easy way for the market researchers to obtain a data file so they can do their own offline data analysis and reporting.

NOTES

LESSON #9

★ ★ ★ ★ ★

VOC PROGRAMS ARE NOT OLD-SCHOOL CSAT TRACKS.

Let's stay on the theme of market research for a moment. Ten-plus years ago, market research firms made big margins on what was called *customer satisfaction tracking*, or CSAT for short. Market research firms often charged millions of dollars for these CSAT programs, and for good reason. Usually on a quarterly basis, they would utilize large telephone interviewing centers for a week or two, calling customers and asking about overall satisfaction levels (usually not most recent experiences). This required a lot of manpower, technical equipment, and overhead.

When VoC software platforms emerged, everything changed. My company, and others in the industry, could now offer the same type of customer satisfaction programs at a third of the cost of previous methods—and deliver results in real time through our software. Suddenly, a client could take immediate action on customer feedback, rather than waiting six to eight weeks on CSAT survey results. CSAT programs quickly became a thing of the past as VoC software platforms took over.

Today, companies get more for their money with VoC. With the ability to send immediate feedback, engage in dialogue with the company, and see quick results, customers have benefited as well. Ideally, companies also have more money to spend on higher-value activities. It's a win for companies, a win for customers, and a win for shareholders.

Perhaps the most important win is reduced hostility between customers and companies. Asking a customer for feedback after a recent experience creates a new touch-point of its own. The experience the customer has *when* they give you feedback influences their perception of your company—plus, no one likes receiving a phone call at dinnertime, as was often the case with CSAT tracks.

With the advancements in VoC software, customer feedback can be collected digitally in a variety of different ways and deliver the results in real time to the entire organization. This phenomenon changed the entire industry, disrupting market research firms and their largest source of reliable, recurring revenue. Now the customer is in charge of whether they want to provide feedback and how they want to provide it. They can fill out an email survey or provide feedback via text, they can offer unsolicited feedback on a social review site—and they can do it all at three in the morning or at six in the evening at their convenience. The customer is in charge!

Compare this approach to how market research firms operated: they called customers according to *their* schedules—whenever their call center employees could work and whatever time period the survey was in the "field."

With VoC, companies respond to individual customer concerns, earn more targeted customers through referrals, and sell more products and services. Market research firms had to pivot to other types of projects as VoC software ate CSAT tracks.

A final word on the difference between CSAT tracks and VoC software: VoC is a third of the cost of a CSAT program via telephone interviewing, and companies can expect ten times more for their money.

If you're still collecting customer feedback through a quarterly generated tracking program via telephone interviewing, it's time to think about the benefits you can gain from VoC—both for your organization and for your customers, as well as for your shareholders.

	CSAT TRACKS	VOC
COST	Very expensive	1/3 cost of CSAT tracks
REACH	Sample of customers	All customers
PRIMARY MODE	Telephone	Online
RESULTS	Weeks	Real time
TIMING	Periodic	Continuous
RESPONDENT EXPERIENCE	Intrusive—on our time	Easy—on the customer's time
ORGANIZATIONAL REACH	Primarily market research	Entire organization
INTERVIEWER BIAS	Yes—results in inflated CSAT scores	None—results in more accurate CSAT scores

CHECKLIST FOR TRANSITIONING FROM CSAT TELEPHONE TRACKS TO VOC SOFTWARE

☐ **Change your mindset.** You might be concerned that you will miss feedback from some of your customers because they do not use email. These days almost everyone has email or a digital way to get in touch with them; you can do this!

☐ **Do an ROI analysis** on what your customer satisfaction tracking program costs, and compare that to a comparable VoC software platform. Take the savings and show it to your CFO. And then ask for a raise.

☐ **Remember that people have a hard time** giving negative feedback to other people. This means that if you are using telephone interviewers to gather customer feedback, your CSAT scores are likely inflated compared to what you will see when you switch to a less biased VoC approach.

- ☐ **Don't use a market research firm to conduct your VoC program.** They are likely licensing or white-labeling VoC software from another company—you will be paying up to double than if you went directly to the VoC software provider!

- ☐ **If you are concerned about getting the reports and insights** that you currently get from your market research provider, there are two solutions—hire an analyst to do this work, and/or engage with a company like PeopleMetrics that provides both VoC software *and* managed services, including strategic reporting.

- ☐ **Operationalize VoC**—now you can give real-time access to customer feedback to people throughout your organization. Make sure you do this, but do it right. More to come on this in Lesson 17.

NOTES

LESSON #10

★ ★ ★ ★ ★

B2*B* VOC AND B2*C* VOC ARE COMPLETELY DIFFERENT.

Who are your customers? Are they businesses (B2B) or consumers (B2C)? The answer to this question is key to creating a world-class VoC program.

B2B companies usually have a smaller number of customers (typically called "clients") who often pay a significant amount for products or services, while B2C companies usually have many customers with a lower comparative price point. A classic example of a large B2B company is Boeing, which sells airplanes to airlines. American Airlines, on the other hand, is primarily a B2C company with millions of customers. Voice of the Customer (or Voice of the Client in the case of B2B companies) is important in both cases, even though the how and why will be different.

A B2B company like Boeing must know about each and every experience a client has with their company, bad or good. An important point is that B2B clients do not provide feedback about their experience through social media. B2B is a relationship business, where commenting on the relationship via online review sites simply does not happen.

In the B2C world, responding to every customer issue reported in a VoC transactional survey is extremely difficult and at times impossible given the potential volume of responses. However, monitoring social media feedback, responding to it, and comparing it to solicited survey feedback is vital! This is especially true for sectors that lend themselves to social reviews, such as hospitality and restaurants.

PRIORITIZING ACTION

So how do B2C companies choose which customers to follow up with when they receive negative feedback from a VoC transactional survey, given the high volume of responses? Enter something called *customer lifetime value*, or CLV for short. CLV is a prediction of the net profit or total revenue attributed to the entire future relationship with a customer. The simple way to calculate CLV is to add together all of the revenue from that customer to date, then project a maximum amount that this customer could provide to the company over time. For example, in the airline industry, customers with the highest CLV are frequent fliers. These customers have spent the most in the past and are most likely to spend more in the future, so keeping them on good terms is key. There is little doubt that losing frequent flyers hurts more than losing an average customer. American Airlines serves so many customers each day that following up with every individual complaint about a rude flight attendant or a broken seat is impossible. But when that negative feedback comes from frequent fliers—passengers with the highest CLV—follow-up is necessary and critical.

While VoC looks different in B2B than in B2C, the idea of using it to retain customers and reduce churn is still central to both. In the B2C world, CLV is used to prioritize follow-ups. Clients in the B2B space, however, almost always have a high CLV. Since losing just one client can be detrimental in the B2B sphere, VoC programs can be an important way to increase communication and check in with all clients.

One word of caution if you are a B2B company: relying solely on VoC for client feedback can create serious problems. There should be a strong, consistent, verbal dialogue between B2B companies and their clients.

Let's say, for instance, you're an accounting firm with

a client that you are billing $250,000 annually. With that account size, both official (i.e., VoC) and unofficial client feedback should be frequent—certainly more than a partner reaching out occasionally or a VoC survey sent periodically. You need both. If you set up VoC touchpoints with that client throughout the year—a kickoff meeting during tax season, a month after the kickoff meeting, two months before taxes are due, and four months before contract renewal—they would allow you to gather feedback throughout the year. In the case of a negative experience, a red flag would be raised, and the situation remedied, before your client decides to leave.

VOC IN BOTH WORLDS

In B2C, business is mainly transactional. There is rarely a salesperson, and when there is one, it's for large-ticket items, such as with electronics, real estate, or automobiles. On the other hand, B2B usually involves people buying from other people. The sales force becomes a key touchpoint in the customer experience for B2B. B2B companies are smart to want to know what their clients think of their sales process and how the expectations that their sales force established compared to their actual experience (see Lesson 20).

While one person, or maybe a couple or a family, makes the final decision in a B2C transaction, there are many decision makers involved in a B2B deal. When American Airlines decides to buy an airplane from Boeing instead of Airbus, they most likely do business with Boeing after an extensive review of alternatives from Airbus, and that decision would likely involve dozens of people. Transactions are so large and expensive that a strong relationship at this level is paramount. Each relationship and each interaction provide touchpoints for VoC feedback in B2B.

Those in B2C need to embrace the fact that they probably have more customer feedback than they know what to do with.

However, the seemingly overwhelming volume of feedback allows B2C companies to learn more about customers and their experiences than ever before. And, through text analytics and other real-time reporting analytical approaches, answers to key questions are immediate. And the more information you have available to you, the more confident you can be in its accuracy. More confidence means you can create better customer experiences.

	B2B	B2C
VOLUME	Small	Large
TEXT ANALYTICS	N/A	Critical
CLOSING LOOPS	Everything/everyone (every client)	CLV prioritizes which customers to follow up with
SOCIAL	N/A	Critical
SALES FORCE	Key touchpoint	Only for large-ticket B2C items
DECISION MAKERS AS PART OF THE PROCESS	Many	Usually 1–2
TRANSACTION SIZE	Expensive/big	Smaller/marginal
SURVEY RESPONSE RATE	15%–30%	5%–10%

CHECKLIST FOR UNDERSTANDING THE DIFFERENCE BETWEEN B2C AND B2B VOC

☐ **First of all, know who you are.** Are you serving businesses or consumers? And if you are serving both, then you need a different VoC program for each. An example of this is banks that have both a retail operation for consumers and commercial operations for businesses.

☐ **Once you are sure who you are serving**, know what you can do and cannot do with VoC.

☐ **If you are B2B, the focus is on understanding and at times responding** to each piece of individual client feedback. You know they are not going on social media to post their comments, and the volume of comments are unlikely to require text analytics to get at what is being said. You also have the all-important sales force touchpoint; don't forget to include this in your VoC program (see Lesson 20)!

- [ ] **If you are B2C, the focus is on the big picture** given the volume of responses you are likely to receive, including any issues that are bubbling up to the top. These are often identified via text analytics (see Lesson 4). You also are unlikely to be able to respond to every customer complaint, so CLV will be key in prioritizing your follow-ups.

- [ ] **Although client feedback can never hurt,** B2B companies with fewer than one hundred clients should think twice before investing in a full-blown VoC program. Instead, they should have formal and regular debriefs with the team servicing those accounts to understand the client experience. However, they should engage in a client relationship survey at least once a year, preferably twice a year.

NOTES

SECTION TWO

WHERE DO YOU START?

LESSON #11

WHERE YOU START WITH VOC DEPENDS ON WHERE YOU ARE.

Every organization has a different level of VoC maturity. Some companies have had VoC in place for many years, while others are just getting started. Companies typically begin in one of three phrases: building, growth, or optimization. Where you start with VoC depends on your level of maturity.

BUILDING PHASE

In the Building Phase, companies either do not have VoC or want to replace their current VoC program and start over. This phase normally lasts a year, and because of its foundational nature, it's an important step.

A good place to start in the Building Phase is with a

relationship survey that asks customers how the overall relationship is going and how their overall experience has been. As reviewed in Lesson 5, NPS is often used in this survey, which helps pinpoint the strength of the customer–company relationship.

After you know where you stand based on the results of the relationship survey, you can then start to put together the building blocks of the core of your VoC program by selecting one touchpoint to focus on with a transactional survey. This first touchpoint is usually easy to determine— it's where you are likely to lose customers and experience churn if you don't get it right. We call this a *moment of truth*, and it is a great place to begin. Moments of truth may involve the contact center or an in-person experience at a retail store or hotel. For a telecommunications firm, a moment of truth might be a home equipment repair visit requiring a technician.

The next step is to figure out how to obtain the customer information needed from that moment of truth, so you can collect customer feedback on that experience. For instance, who in your organization has the information about home visits by a technician? We are talking about specific information here—customer name, email address, time/date of visit, name of technician who provided service. After that, it is key to determine how to get that customer information into your VoC software platform so surveys can automatically go out after a recent visit to the home.

From here, you can progress to goal setting. Goals usually include either overall customer satisfaction or NPS. Another common goal is a certain percentage of surveys that contain a problem identified by a customer (in that case, the goal would be to have a score that is as low as possible). The final step in the Building Phase is identifying a sponsor. This is someone at the company who is passionate about CX, fully supports VoC, and will commit to seeing the process through. Think company president or CEO for this role—you need their momentum before you can move into the next phase.

A key part of the Building Phase is to remember that if this is the first time your company has implemented VoC, you need to rely on experts to guide you. Find an individual or organization, in-house or an outside partner, who knows the right questions to ask to the right customers at the right time. An expert can help you identify that moment of truth touchpoint, communicate what's going on to employees and key stakeholders, help you understand the initial results, and identify which findings should be shared with whom and when. Don't do all of this yourself—a good partner will save you time and money.

GROWTH PHASE

The first year of VoC is spent setting a foundation and starting to gather continuous customer feedback. In the second and third years, the fun part starts: actually helping improve CX and seeing the business results that follow. In the Building Phase, you might have set a goal for NPS. Rather than just monitoring these goals, you can now assign accountability for achieving them. For a hospitality company, you might assign a specific NPS goal to the general manager at each of your hotels. Once achieved, these targets could factor into a manager's annual bonus (see Lesson 35).

You've had a year or more of VoC data and can now be confident in your targets. A year's worth of customer feedback can build a model that is accurate and full of usable information. For example, text analytics can now be applied, making sense of qualitative (unstructured) feedback in real time (see Lesson 4). This is also the time to consider adding touchpoints, channels, or locations to add breadth to the program. If you look at the Growth Phase in the earlier telecommunications company example, you might add installation and contact center review touchpoints to the initial "moment of truth" touchpoint of repair work.

Everyone in the organization should now have access to the customer feedback results via your VoC software platform. Maybe only a small slice was ready for everyone in the Building Phase, but in the Growth Phase, the whole pie is available. Everyone responsible for a touchpoint can now analyze the customer experience to determine what's going right and what's going wrong. Those on the front line not only have access to this data but can also use it to close the loop, follow up with customers who had negative experiences, and reduce churn.

The Growth Phase is where the culture of an organization begins to change. Everybody at the company knows about VoC. They can log in to review information and see reports, or they might hear about it directly from executives at town hall meetings. Healthy competition can be sparked between departments or locations to help the organization exceed NPS targets, creating a strong customer-centric culture.

OPTIMIZATION PHASE

In the Optimization Phase, the newness is over. This is often the most challenging phase. After three years, some people might even be fatigued from all this customer feedback! However, this phase also provides you with your best opportunity for using customer feedback to drive business results and continued reshaping of the organizational culture to focus on the customer.

In the Building Phase, you learned how to get the customer information you need to send out surveys in a timely manner. In the Growth Phase, you automated the process and involved the entire organization. Now, in the Optimization Phase, you have the opportunity to integrate customer feedback with operational systems. For example, customer feedback can be integrated within business intelligence tools—which run analytics on organizational data and report on the findings. Financial data from other systems might also be integrated in order to build a case for the ROI of the customer experience. For example, how much churn did the VoC program really prevent? How many positive social reviews did the program generate? How many new leads did the program generate, and how many of them led to new business?

In this phase, you may no longer rely on a partner or consultant to figure out pitfalls and help you manage your VoC software platform. You can manage the users, create new dashboards, and analyze the data in-house. There may be a full department at your organization dedicated to VoC, and most likely, they're making it work. It's no longer a one-man show—after three years, this commitment requires manpower. Typically, this becomes the customer experience department, and it's a legitimate and substantial part of the organization. Benchmarking becomes increasingly important so that you can understand where your company stands in comparison to competitors. Internal benchmarks are also key here as you understand what is considered "best of breed" within your organization.

Now that VoC is well known throughout the company, other departments will want to add their own strategic questions to the core transactional VoC survey. The market research department, for instance, knows about this continuous stream of customer feedback, and they may want to know what customers think of a new menu item, logo, or pricing structure (see Lesson 8).

With all this data and increased sophistication, various analytical tools become available. Text analytics becomes more accurate in this phase as it's accessed more frequently by employees. There are now algorithms available that can tell the general manager of a hotel what they need to focus on next in order to improve the customer experience in their hotel (see Lesson 38). ROI analysis is necessary in the Optimization Phase because the sponsor from the Building Phase now wants to see if VoC is worth continuing to invest in. Is there evidence that the program is working enough to justify the investment?

You also know now how much the customer experience has improved (or diminished) since the implementation of VoC.

CHECKLIST FOR BUILDING THE RIGHT VOC PROGRAM DEPENDING ON WHERE YOU ARE

- ☐ **First of all, identify where you are.** Are you starting from scratch with no VoC in place? Or is there a VoC in place that's not working? Or are you two, three, four, or ten years into VoC?
- ☐ **Wherever you are, you have an opportunity to build** an amazing VoC that will deliver ROI and change the fabric of your organization for the better.
- ☐ If you are in the Building Phase (i.e., no program or one in place you want to replace):
  - ☐ **Start slow and ease into VoC.** Rely on a trusted partner who knows VoC, has great software, and can help you avoid common mistakes.
  - ☐ **Start with a relationship survey** to get a baseline on your NPS as well as identify where you are doing well and need improvement.
  - ☐ **Identify where your customer transactional information is stored**—this is key to actually gathering customer feedback.
  - ☐ **Begin your transactional VoC survey** with one key touchpoint called a *moment of truth* where if you don't get it right, the customer will leave you and/or speak badly about you.
  - ☐ **Finally, you must identify a sponsor or champion** for VoC in this phase, ideally someone higher up within the organization.

- [ ] If you are in the exciting Growth Phase (i.e., two to three years in):
  - [ ] **Lean on your VoC partner even more** than ever to help you turbocharge your VoC.
  - [ ] **Identify specific goals for your program,** including who is accountable for achieving these goals.
  - [ ] **Tie bonus compensation** to achieving these goals.
  - [ ] **Open up VoC results to the entire company,** especially those who are responsible for a given touchpoint.
  - [ ] **Include additional touchpoints in this phase,** making sure you are getting feedback on the most critical parts of the customer journey.
  - [ ] **Don't forget to bask in the glow** of watching your organization really become more customer-centric as more and more people get access to and respond to customer feedback on a daily basis. This is truly an amazing time.
- [ ] If you are in the Optimization Phase:
  - [ ] **Remember that your work is incredibly important** in this phase, but it might seem like progress is incremental.
  - [ ] **Get your ROI hat on**—you will get questions on why you are continuing to invest in VoC. The irony is that this is when the ROI is often the highest. You are likely now able to connect VoC data into other systems such as CRM, business intelligence,

and financial. As a result, CX data is leveraged and more powerful now than in any other phase.

☐ **Make sure you are leveraging your benchmarks** to compare performance to other companies as well as internal "best of breed" locations or groups.

☐ **Check to see if you can take on some or all** of the managed services provided by your VoC partner—you or your team can now add users, create new dashboards, add market research questions via hot swaps, do your own analysis, and more.

NOTES

LESSON #12

NO MATTER WHERE YOU ARE OR WHAT INDUSTRY YOU ARE IN, GET LEADERSHIP TO BUY IN, OR DON'T BOTHER WITH VOC.

The absolute number one requirement for VoC to work in any organization is buy-in from the leadership team. Specifically, an executive or CEO must serve as a sponsor and show support for CX and the business impact of regularly listening to customers. Without this support, no company can be customer-centric for the long haul.

There should be at least one executive sponsor who genuinely cares about VoC. This can be the CEO, CMO, and/or COO. Their buy-in means they are willing to invest in VoC and allocate resources to it. They should be willing to hire someone to serve as head of customer experience and VoC. You want the sponsor to talk about the importance of VoC with the entire company—CX as both a topic and a department should have a seat at the table in important company meetings.

Without leadership buy-in and an executive sponsor, the organization as a whole will not be excited about VoC, understand their role, or even know why listening to customers is important. Without a strong sponsor, VoC is often led by market research. When that happens, VoC's results rarely hit the front line, where the biggest difference can be made in terms of improving the customer experience and reducing churn. In this situation, the results are often questioned—if an executive doesn't believe in VoC and receives negative feedback, they tend to doubt the results and the benefits. The focus becomes protecting the company's operations rather than improving the customer experience. Without proper investment—in terms of both finances and support—the programs die out or stay so small that they cannot be effective.

Please note that a sponsor leaving the company can be as disastrous for VoC as much as not having support to begin with. If the sponsor is not replaced quickly, the entire organization often loses interest. Customer feedback is collected, but no one reviews it or acts on it. VoC might continue for a while on autopilot but is usually canceled. It may resurface if a sponsor picks it up and assigns resources to it, but this is not guaranteed to happen.

CHECKLIST FOR MAKING SURE VOC WON'T FAIL OUT OF THE GATES

- ☐ **Secure an executive sponsor** of VoC, or it will fail.
- ☐ **Start with the CEO** and then work your way to the COO, CMO...it needs to be someone on the leadership team whom the entire organization respects.
- ☐ **Use that executive sponsor** to market VoC internally—have the sponsor send out company-wide communication on VoC, have town-hall-style talks about VoC...really anything you can do to add credibility and weight to the program.
- ☐ **Make sure the executive sponsor speaks** of the powerful business impact of VoC—that it will help your company reduce churn, improve your social profile, and even generate new leads for the sales team that result in increased revenue.
- ☐ **If your executive sponsor departs the company or is reassigned,** move as quickly as possible to secure a replacement sponsor. If you do not, VoC is in danger.

NOTES

LESSON #13

ROI IS EVERYTHING. GAIN LEADERSHIP BUY-IN FOR VOC BY SHOWING THEM THE $$$.

For almost any initiative in business, the way to convince leadership to invest is to show them a return on investment. In turn, the best way to secure executive sponsorship in VoC is to demonstrate that improving the customer experience pays big returns. In other words, you need to create a business case for investing in improving CX and, in turn, regularly listening to your customers via VoC.

As the head of the customer experience team, begin by gathering statistics and public information about companies that have invested in the customer experience and have seen a return on that investment, then begin to create your own internal business case for VoC.

There are a plethora of publicly available studies and reports available for you to use to bolster your case. Here are a few to get you started:

1. Temkin Group (www.temkingroup.com) has excellent research in this area, including a study called "Economics of Net Promoter Score" (2017) that provides ample evidence that NPS yields tangible business results, including the ability to upsell customers who will recommend you.

2. Forrester (www.forrester.com) has a must-read report called "Why CX? Why Now?" (2016) that provides compelling ROI evidence that CX matters, including the ability to charge a higher price when you deliver a better customer experience.

3. Watermark Consulting (www.watermarkconsult. net), a US-based customer experience advisory firm, analyzed the stock market returns of the Top 10 and Bottom 10 publicly traded companies in Forrester's Customer Experience Index. Over the long term, a portfolio of those Customer Experience Leader firms far outperformed their Laggard counterparts. In industry-specific studies, they also showed that this relationship between CX excellence and stock market performance held up in both the auto insurance and home insurance markets. I've included three diagrams for details.

Customer Experience Leaders Outperform the Market

8-Year Stock Performance of Customer Experience Leaders vs. Laggards vs. S&P 500 (2007-2014)

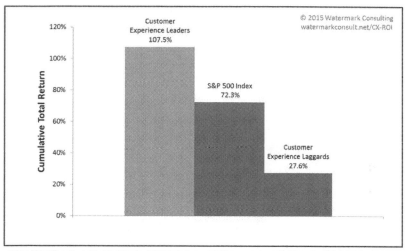

Watermark defines Customer Experience Leaders and Laggards as the top ten and bottom ten rated public companies in Forrester Research's 2007-2015 Customer Experience Index studies. Comparison is based on performance of equally-weighted, annually readjusted stock portfolios of Customer Experience Leaders and Laggards relative to the S&P 500 Index.

Customer Experience Leaders Outperform the Market
An Auto Insurance Industry View

7-Year Stock Performance of Auto Insurance Customer Experience Leaders vs. Laggards (2009-2015)

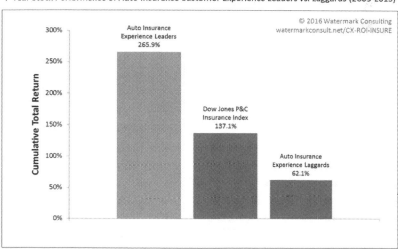

Watermark defines Auto Insurance Customer Experience Leaders and Laggards as the publicly-traded insurers falling in the Top 5 and Bottom 5 national ranking of J.D. Power's 2010-2016 U.S. Auto Insurance Satisfaction Studies. Comparison is based on performance of equally-weighted, annually readjusted stock portfolios of Customer Experience Leaders and Laggards.

Customer Experience Leaders Outperform the Market
A Home Insurance Industry View
8-Year Stock Performance of Home Insurance Customer Experience Leaders vs. Laggards (2008-2015)

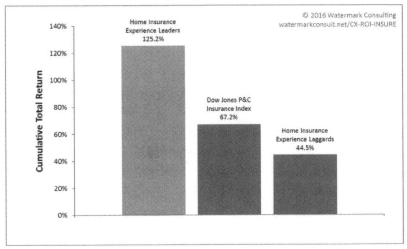

Watermark defines Home Insurance Customer Experience Leaders and Laggards as the Top 5 and Bottom 5 publicly traded insurers in J.D. Power's 2009-2016 U.S. Home Insurance Studies. Comparison is based on performance of equally weighted, annually readjusted stock portfolios of Customer Experience Leaders and Laggards.

LOOK INSIDE AT CLV TO DETERMINE ROI

Public information is the first place to begin and often the only place to start if you have no VoC in place. But if you have VoC running, your ROI possibilities are much greater. You can examine your own VoC data to build out a ROI case specific to your company. Let's take a hypothetical example where you are the head of CX for a B2B telecommunications company. Here's one way you can go about building an ROI case with internal data:

1. Determine the customer lifetime value for each of your average clients, or the average revenue you can expect from the client—say, on average, $100,000 per client.

2. Identify fifty clients who had a problem or concern that you were made aware of through VoC. You can prove ROI in this small-scale study without contacting all your customers. This small pilot study—with a limited budget—carries so much potential for proving ROI that most executives will fund it. Continuing the example, let's say billing was inaccurate and hard to understand. Maybe the customer had a difficult time adding and deleting phones, and their changes never showed up accurately on their bill. Without VoC, your organization may not have known about this situation. Contracts end, and it's easy for an unhappy customer to give thirty days' notice with no warning. The customer might have tried to resolve the issue with the less-than-empathetic billing department before simply giving up. On the other hand, if the problem is identified via VoC and someone from the customer experience team follows up with the client, the situation can be turned around before the client cancels. Maybe the customer experience team needs to facilitate a resolution with the billing department so that statements read more clearly, or maybe they need to find a way to improve the process of adding and deleting phones. Either way, their job is to find a resolution and save the customer. At $100,000 a pop, it's not hard to justify this work.

3. Assume that 10 percent of clients would have gone to a competitor if you or your team had not followed

up and resolved the issue. Five out of fifty customers may not sound like a lot, but when you consider that each brings in $100,000 of revenue over their lifetime, the benefit of VoC becomes a no-brainer. It's $500,000 saved in churn compared to whatever you are investing in VoC.

4. A more precise approach to quantifying the ROI impact of closing the loop with those fifty customers is to do a follow-up survey that we call a *Full Circle Survey* at PeopleMetrics (see Lesson 30). In this survey, we ask customers if the issue was resolved and if their perceptions of the company improved.

CHECKLIST FOR CREATING A KILLER ROI CASE FOR CX AND VOC

☐ **Nothing gains executive buy-in and budget** expansion than a solid ROI case.

☐ **Your main job is to build a case study for why CX matters**, why investing in CX will result in an ROI for the company, and indirectly why measuring CX via VoC is a sound investment for the company. If you can't do this, you won't get initial funding for VoC or a budget over time to grow the program.

☐ **Start with publicly available studies** on the power and impact of CX on financial results. There are plenty of public studies available, including several by Watermark Consulting, Temkin Group, and Forrester. This is likely where you need to begin and end if you are just starting VoC. The goal here is to secure the executive sponsor and obtain the budget to at least begin to pilot VoC.

- [ ] **The primary driver of ROI for VoC for most companies is reduction in churn.** Make sure you home in on this one and point out evidence that customer feedback enables the organization to retain customers for the long haul.

- [ ] **If social reviews are important to your industry** (e.g., hotels, restaurants), show how many positive social reviews were a result of VoC survey participants being "pushed" to social review sites after they were finished with the survey. Positive social reviews are gold in certain industries (see Lesson 29).

- [ ] **Make sure you point to any leads** that get generated as result of your VoC—transactional VoC surveys can be set up to ask the customer if they are interested in additional products and services that you offer. Track the amount of new revenue generated by upselling customers.

- [ ] **If you are B2B, have your sales team follow up** on each and every "promoter" (see Lesson 30) to thank them for providing the feedback and then ask for a referral. Track the amount of new revenue generated by these referrals.

- [ ] **Remember, just because you got initial funding** for VoC does not mean your job is over; you must continually show ROI over time. This is why having ROI on your mind at all times is vital!

☐ **If you have VoC running**, you have the opportunity to create a custom ROI analysis. The key here is to start simple and build your case. Key variables include customer lifetime value (CLV), current churn rate, number of problems identified via VoC, and number of follow-ups done by the internal team with customers who had issues.

☐ **A Full Circle Survey is an excellent approach** to pinpointing the ROI of closing the loop with customers after they have an issue. Use this approach as part of your ROI strategy.

NOTES

LESSON #14

COMMUNICATE, COMMUNICATE, COMMUNICATE—TO ALL INTERNAL STAKEHOLDERS— OR YOU WILL REGRET IT.

You have presented an ROI case, may have acquired the budget to pilot VoC, and have earned the commitment of an executive sponsor who supports VoC. Congratulations! Your job is just beginning.

Once you have resources and sponsorship, communication is the next make-or-break element of a successful VoC program. As the head of the customer experience team, your responsibility is first to motivate, encourage, and engage the sponsor to regularly communicate with key stakeholders—the others at the organization who are impacted by this process. You can and should own follow-up communication yourself.

A great program communicator has the same mindset as a marketing professional. You have to think about marketing VoC to your organization the same way you would market a new product or service to your customers. At the onset of the program, communicate what VoC is, why it's important, how it will drive business results, and what touchpoints you will focus on.

I've seen companies do actual internal marketing campaigns, with posters in every office, intranet articles and blog posts written by executives, and town hall meetings—complete with skits demonstrating good and bad customer experiences!

Once VoC has begun, companies often share results with the entire organization. This is typically done by turning online dashboards and offline analytics into huge, colorful posters! This way, every employee knows the company's NPS, the number of problems experienced by customers, and the speed at which teams were able to solve them. Employees see the positive and negative experiences reported by customers, and with so many bright posters lighting up the office, they are excited and informed!

Some of our clients also have daily or weekly team briefings to keep everyone current with what's going on with the customer experience and VoC.

For example, Signature Flight Support is a client of ours that services private jets at a variety of locations all over the world. They do everything from fueling and servicing the planes to hosting a lounge for pilots and passengers. Each day, at 158 of their locations, they review the customer feedback from the prior day. In some cases, they review every single survey from the previous day—both the positive and negative—and use the feedback to improve their service that day. When a customer provides positive feedback about a particular employee, that employee is congratulated in the daily briefing that each location has every morning. When there's a problem, it's followed up on immediately, and it's discussed as a team so they can determine how they can prevent it from happening in the future.

Once customer feedback via VoC begins to roll in, you are not done! Communication must continue. Users need to know how to log in to your VoC software platform and how to handle customer complaints about a recent experience. They need to know how to open these cases, how to use email templates to follow up, and when a phone call to the customer will be necessary. It's also important that they know what they are authorized to do to save the customer—for example, can they provide a discount or a free product?

Once again, if there was any doubt about the difference

between VoC and market research, the communication element should make this difference clear. Market researchers are centrally located in one department. One person or team will initiate the study, collect data, analyze the results, and present the results to a few people within the organization. VoC is operational and touches the whole organization, including those delivering the service or supporting the customer.

CHECKLIST FOR BEING A VOC COMMUNICATIONS NINJA

- ☐ **Think of yourself as a marketer** within your organization. Your job is to get the message out and "sell" your organization on the value of VoC.
- ☐ **Getting your executive sponsor engaged** and out there communicating is key to making VoC successful. You or someone on your team may have to schedule these communications. You might even have to craft what the sponsor says. It's all worth it.
- ☐ **You should communicate yourself**! Make sure you are quickly following up your executive sponsor and reinforcing their messages.
- ☐ **Posters, videos, blog posts, town hall meetings**, podcasts, Slack messages, etc., are all fair game in terms of VoC communication tactics.
- ☐ **Once VoC is off the ground**, make sure you and your team are sharing the results on a regular basis! Get

creative—take key online dashboards and blow them up into huge posters and put them on the walls. Create entertaining skits where you show what a great customer experience looks like and what a terrible one looks like...based on actual customer feedback.

☐ **Get your communication to scale** by encouraging daily huddles for teams responsible for CX. Many of PeopleMetrics' clients do this daily by reviewing the prior day's customer feedback, determining which customers to follow up with, and celebrating any employee who helped deliver a great CX!

NOTES

SECTION THREE

———

ASK FOR HELP

LESSON #15

YOU CAN'T DO THIS ALL YOURSELF. YOU WILL NEED HELP INTERNALLY.

No matter how talented you are as a customer experience professional, you need a team to create a world-class VoC program. In this lesson, I am focusing on the internal help you will need. In Lesson 16, I will focus on external partners.

Let's begin with the information technology department (IT). IT should be your best friend in making VoC happen—as long as you keep an eye on the costs.

The reason is that IT controls the most up-to-date information you need about the customer experience. In a telecommunications company, for example, the IT department has a system that houses all the technician appointments for the day, including specific customer information such as email address and phone number. They can also tell you how long someone has been a customer, how much they pay for service each month, and their billing trend over time.

As the lead of the customer experience team, you have to be multifunctional, with the right mindset and communication skills to connect with different personalities. This will help when interacting with your IT department. You'll have to be incredibly specific about what you need. If you allow an IT department to lead the conversation about VoC, the bill will likely be too high and the timeline will probably take too long. IT might say, "That's not possible" when what that really means is "I don't want to do that."

At PeopleMetrics, we once partnered with a client on a VoC program, and their IT department was asked to provide a list of customers who had a recent experience with the company. When IT came back to our client contact, the VP of customer experience, they introduced a $2 million bill—five times the amount of the entire VoC program! Their IT group had a limited understanding of our VoC software platform and its capabilities. On behalf of our client, we returned to IT with a narrow request of what we needed. Once they understood our specific needs, the cost was nominal, and the time frame was fast.

The minimum support you need from IT is something called a *flat file*. This is often an Excel or CSV file that contains a list of customers who recently had an experience with the company. Once you specify how frequently you need this information to be collected—such as daily, twice a day, or weekly—then you can upload the customer information into your VoC software platform so surveys can be sent out. IT can also help create an automated system for this process, such as connecting a point-of-sale system or CRM to your VoC software platform via an API. This automated process does not require you or your team to upload files or to always check the accuracy of the files or the upload.

In addition to IT, you'll need assistance to help you understand what all of this customer feedback means. Sometimes, you're fortunate to have your own analyst, but in the Building Phase or even the Growth Phase, this is rarely the case. If your company has a business analytics and business intelligence department, they can be very helpful in connecting the dots and making sense of customer feedback.

The other internal departments that you will likely need to interact with are legal and procurement. At times, legal will need to approve questions that get asked to customers. This is especially true in highly regulated industries, such as pharmaceuticals. Legal will also come into play if you decide to engage with a third-party partner (more on that in Lesson 16). Legal can help you create a contract with that partner. A related department, procurement, may also get involved if you decide to go out to "bid" for VoC software and services. This group will help you craft a Response for Proposal (RFP) that you can send out to multiple VoC providers. Procurement will help you ask the right questions, consolidate responses, choose the right partner, and negotiate the cost/terms of the program.

CHECKLIST FOR GETTING THE INTERNAL HELP YOU NEED

- ☐ **Start with IT**; this is your most important internal group that you will need to get VoC off the ground. IT usually controls the customer information you will need to send out a timely survey after a recent customer experience.
- ☐ **While IT is vital,** don't let them walk all over you. Keep a keen eye on costs. Make sure your requests to IT are super specific and unambiguous.
- ☐ **Business intelligence is another group** that is worth their weight in gold. They can provide help with analyzing your CX results and make sense of the findings. Your job is to often tell a story to executives about what is happening with the customer experience. This group can help you tell this story better.
- ☐ **You will need legal in order to create contracts** with

external partners that you may need to execute VoC. They may also be needed to approve questions you ask to customers.

☐ **Procurement can help you select external VoC partners** and negotiate the cost and terms.

NOTES

CHANCES ARE YOU NEED HELP FROM THE OUTSIDE TO GET THIS DONE—DO YOU NEED A SURVEY TOOL OR A VOC PARTNER?

Unless you're working in a small company, the full spectrum of VoC responsibilities are usually too much for one person. You might think you can create a world-class VoC yourself using a low-end technology tool, but this can be risky, especially in the Building Phase. In the beginning, your best chance at success is to partner with an organization that has done this before, is an expert in VoC, and can help you get off to a good start. This expense will pay for itself ten times over.

When you purchase a tool, you're buying software licenses so that your team can configure and manage VoC. In this scenario, you figure out the touchpoints and the questions to ask customers. You create dashboards that your stakeholders review, and you add user credentials. You are responsible for managing the whole process as well as analyzing the data and organizing it into artifacts (usually PowerPoint decks) to present to the executive team. It is a really heavy lift.

FINDING OUTSIDE HELP

In most cases, you are going to need a VoC partner to help you. Your first decision is this: Do you want a firm that is an *order taker* or a *value-added provider*? If your VoC program is more mature or you have experienced CX and VoC resources at your disposal, then an order taker that executes flawlessly makes sense. If you are just starting out or your industry has gone through rapid change, partnering with a firm that can provide expertise within CX and VoC will be well worth the investment.

No matter what, your VoC partner should certainly have an implementation team that sets up your VoC, including survey design, programming, dashboard creation, user setup, and ensuring your customer list is ready to go once you are ready to begin. People within your organization must be able to log in and see their VoC data and results—if they can't, they need to be able to call someone to help them, and that someone cannot be you! As the customer experience lead, you need to focus on how to improve the customer experience rather than managing a complex software process and providing technical support.

A good value-added VoC partner can also help you identify specific things you can do immediately to improve the customer experience. It's difficult to review VoC data by yourself in the beginning, and to understand what is really important and to tell a story as to what is going on with CX within your company. With a value-added VoC partner, you can be confident that your program will work well from the start.

A value-added VoC partner is also helpful when you run into the challenges that you will inevitably face. For example, when your partner is able to speak the language of IT, this will save you countless hours and potential roadblocks. The bottom line is that experienced partners can be invaluable.

As the leader of CX at your company, you need to focus on what you do well and not get bogged down by tactical details that a value-added VoC partner can handle. You were not hired to be an expert in VoC program design and software configuration. Your unique ability is being the customer advocate for the organization, identifying ways to improve the customer experience across the enterprise, and ensuring business results are positively impacted.

A final word on the value of a good VoC partner: do not discount the power of telling a good story to your executives around how your customers are feeling and what you can do now to improve the customer experience. At

PeopleMetrics, not only do we help our clients design a world-class VoC, but we also help tell the story via various analytical techniques. Our goal is always to make our clients the heroes of their organization by arming them with CX stories that they can share with their VoC sponsor and the entire organization.

The CX story you tell executives must reinforce the program's ROI. And be specific. How many customers has the VoC program saved? How many positive social reviews has it generated? How many new business leads have been generated as a result of VoC? If this step is not taken, ROI will be more difficult to prove in the future, and the program will become little more than a data collection exercise.

Another type of outside help to consider is training your company on the basics of delivering a great customer experience. The DiJulius Group (www.thedijuliusgroup. com) does an excellent job with both in-person and online CX training. I find that having employees trained on *how* to deliver a great CX makes them much more engaged with VoC and more likely to want to improve over time.

CHECKLIST FOR FINDING A VOC PARTNER

This is a special checklist that contains a few of the key questions you should ask prospective VoC partners:

- [ ] **How will you help us** drive business results from VoC?
- [ ] **Do you provide both** VoC software *and* implementation services?
- [ ] **What do your implementation services include?** Will you help us with more than software configuration, including touchpoint mapping, survey design, dashboard design, and user training?
- [ ] **Do you provide ongoing managed services,** including strategic reporting that provides a summary of how we are doing and recommendations for improvement?
- [ ] **Who will be your day-to-day contact?** Is this person an expert in CX/VoC?
- [ ] **Do you offer text analytics** as part of your VoC software platform? If so, is your text analytics native (i.e., developed in-house), or do you license a third-party product?
- [ ] **Do you charge per user** who accesses your VoC software platform, or do you have an unlimited user model?
- [ ] **If you do not price per user,** how do you price your software and services? Is this by location, touchpoint, or some other method?
- [ ] **How secure and scalable** is your software platform? Are you hosting your own servers, or are you using Amazon Web Services (AWS) or a similar back-end solution?
- [ ] **Is your software self-service capable?** Can we set up users, create dashboards, and design surveys ourselves, or do we need to ask you to do this for us? If you do this for us, how much will you charge?

NOTES

BUILD A GREAT SURVEY

LESSON #17

THE SURVEY IS DEAD. LONG LIVE THE SURVEY!

There is a great debate in the CX world about the future of surveys. No one doubts the importance of listening to customers; the debate centers on if the survey as we know it is the best way to enable that.

What we do know is that survey response rates are declining. It seems like people complain about being bombarded with surveys. For these reasons, it's a commonly held belief that the survey's days are numbered. But is that true?

In reality, more surveys are sent and completed than ever before due to the ease and cost-effectiveness of online surveys. Hotels, restaurants, and retail stores distribute them regularly, but so do a plethora of other industries, including banking, insurance, car repair, and many more.

Despite their challenges, surveys are still the easiest and most cost-effective way for a customer to provide feedback about their experience.

Surveys get a bad rap for two reasons. First, many are way too long. Some can take thirty minutes or more to complete and require people to be on a laptop or desktop, since completing a long survey on a mobile device is difficult. Let's be clear that a longer survey is not or at least should not be considered VoC, at least not in the way I am describing it in this book. But even VoC surveys that take longer than a few minutes are rarely successful, given that most customers taking them on mobile devices will give up after just a minute or two. Just five years ago at PeopleMetrics, almost no one completed our surveys from a mobile device. Now, 75% of surveys are completed this way. This is not just a PeopleMetrics thing; it's a major industry shift.

Second, organizations send out too many surveys to the same customer, leading to "survey fatigue." The first problem (long surveys) is not generally a VoC issue, but this one certainly is. Companies, in their enthusiasm to gather customer feedback on various touchpoints, often do not implement checks and balances that ensure that any one customer is not over-surveyed.

One strategy to prevent this is what we call the *month rule* at PeopleMetrics. The month rule prevents any customer from receiving a survey invitation more than once every thirty days. Some clients extend this rule to every sixty or ninety days, depending on their business and volume of customer interactions.

Another strategy to reduce survey fatigue among your customers is to get control of the "rogue" survey senders within your own organization. A common circumstance is that folks in marketing, market research, strategy, or operations will commission their own survey without your knowledge. So they create a survey (usually via SurveyMonkey), make friends with IT to get a customer list (probably the same one you are using), and then send surveys to these customers. The result is yet another survey sent to the same customers you are engaging on a continuous basis in your VoC program! The solution is to make your VoC software platform the central hub and single source of truth for all customer feedback (see Lesson 3). This will require you to corral these rogue survey senders and ensure all customer feedback is centralized within your team and your VoC software platform. It is hard work but well worth it!

THE RIGHT SURVEY AT THE RIGHT TIME

While not perfect, surveys are here to stay, and they will be a key part of 99% of all VoC programs. The real question is not "Is the survey dying?" but "Which are the best surveys to use for your VoC?"

As mentioned in Lesson 2, the two types of surveys used in VoC programs are *relationship surveys* and *transactional surveys*. A relationship survey is one that you send to all customers to gauge the strength of the overall relationship, while a transactional survey is sent immediately after a recent customer experience to understand how the latest interactions with customers are going.

RELATIONSHIP SURVEYS

A relationship survey is used to take a snapshot of a company's relationship with their customers. Questions are focused on getting customer feedback on experiences across all touchpoints.

The first question in a relationship survey is almost always NPS. Customers are asked to complete a relationship survey over a one- to two-week fielding period, and it usually takes about fifteen minutes to complete. As mentioned previously, the goal here is not to determine if a recent experience is good or bad. The focus is on where you are overall with your customers and more about *why* people are having great experiences or negative experiences with a company in general.

Perhaps the best thing about relationship surveys is that they can be completed quickly, and they don't need to involve the entire organization. Usually, the only people seeing the relationship survey results are the program sponsors—such as the head of customer experience, the head of marketing, and the head of operations. Relationship surveys can be a quick win—requiring little time and providing valuable information.

TRANSACTIONAL SURVEYS

Transactional surveys are conducted immediately after a customer experience. Typical examples include after shopping at a retail store, checking out of a hotel, or dining at a restaurant. These questions are not about the customer's overall relationship with the company, but the *most recent* customer experience. Transactional surveys are the core of most VoC survey programs.

Unlike relationship surveys, transactional surveys are brief, lasting anywhere from two to five minutes and collecting information quickly after the experience or, at times, *during the experience*! More on "in-moment" surveys is in Lesson 40.

TURNING SURVEYS INTO ACTION

In their outstanding book *Outside In: The Power of Putting*

Customers at the Center of Your Business, authors Harley Manning and Kerry Bodine do an excellent job of focusing on how relationship surveys are a key part of being customer-centric. What we are adding here is operationalizing VoC through transactional surveys where the entire organization gains access to results.

VoC is more than relationship surveys. They are certainly the beginning of a best-in-class VoC, but the operational side—the side where data is democratized so every front-line person can access it—is vital. Otherwise, you simply have a high-level overview of customer snapshots, reminiscent of market research. Without consistent action to improve the customer experience on a daily basis, you really aren't creating a modern VoC program.

Let's use an example to illustrate. Say you want to get in good physical shape and lose twenty-five pounds by the end of the year. In January, you work really hard for a week, exercising daily. But after the week is up, you lose interest and stop working out. The result is that you are unlikely to hit your goal. The only way to lose the twenty-five pounds is with consistent activity throughout the week and, ultimately, throughout the year. The customer experience works on the same principle.

Customer experience should be measured every day so that your team is empowered to not only access the data but also to act on it to improve the customer experience and drive business results. The goal is daily improvement by fixing specific customer problems. VoC is really about consistently collecting transactional customer feedback, delivering this feedback to the people on the front lines who provide the customer experience, and empowering them to act on it. Period.

One final word: it's always better to do something instead of nothing. Exercising for the month of January is better than not exercising at all. Likewise, taking occasional customer snapshots via a relationship survey is better than never asking customers what they think—but sporadic activity will not create lasting change or create a customer-centric organization.

	RELATIONSHIP	TRANSACTIONAL
LENGTH	Longer (10–15 mins; 50 questions)	Short (2–5 minutes, 5–15 questions)
FREQUENCY	Once or twice a year	Continuous
PURPOSE	Strategic baseline	Operational improvement
OUTCOME MEASURE	Net Promoter Score (NPS)	Overall satisfaction with most recent experience
RESULTS AUDIENCE	Sponsor of program	Distributed across organization (everyone)
INCENTIVE	Individual incentive common	Either no incentive or sweepstakes
CUSTOMER TYPE	Anyone who is a customer over the past 6–12 months	Customer who has had a recent experience via any touchpoint
COST	One-time cost with (30k–50k) or without analysis (12k)	Monthly cost (2k+ a month)
ANALYSIS	Immediately after fielding	Requires a quarter to obtain enough customer responses
ALERTS	Not ideal/not timely	Live, rolling, expected

CHECKLIST FOR SURVEY GREATNESS

☐ **Remember that in the world of VoC, surveys are still** the most viable method to collect customer feedback.

☐ **The two types of surveys relevant to VoC** are relationship surveys and transactional surveys.

☐ **A relationship survey is a great starting point** to build your VoC program—it's quick (in and out of the field in two weeks), it does not require you to involve other people/departments outside of IT or whoever can get you a reliable customer list, and there is no need to follow up on individual customer issues (unless you want to).

☐ **A transactional survey is really the heart** of your VoC program, because it allows you to operationalize the customer feedback throughout your organization. This often means following up with individual customers who have had a poor experience and holding people accountable for achieving certain levels of CX success (usually through the form of incentive compensation).

☐ **Surveys need to be** as long as they need to be but no longer. Transactional surveys should be two to five minutes, while relationship surveys should be more like ten to fifteen minutes.

☐ **Survey fatigue is real,** and you need to remember the two key strategies to avoid this. The first is the month rule, which prevents individual customers from receiving a survey more than once every thirty days (or sixty or ninety, depending on your business). The second is making VoC the single source of truth for all your customer feedback. This requires you to round up "rogue" survey senders within your organization and coordinate all customer feedback within your platform.

NOTES

LESSON #18

USE CUSTOMER TOUCHPOINT MAPPING TO GET TO THE RIGHT SURVEY QUESTIONS, BUT DON'T BOIL THE OCEAN.

Whether you start with a relationship survey or a transactional survey, you need to know which touchpoint(s) to focus on. Enter touchpoint mapping, a concept I introduced in Lesson 7, when I was pointing out the difference between customer service and customer experience. Now we are going to go into this concept a little deeper.

Touchpoint mapping is simply identifying all the possible touches or interactions you have with your customers. Let's walk through how this might work in the hospitality industry. How does a hotel guest interact with a hotel, from the beginning of the experience to the end? The main touchpoints are likely as follows:

1. **Digital:** Most likely, they land on the hotel's webpage first—whether that's through a website like booking. com, a TripAdvisor review, or a direct Google search inquiry—where the customer figures out everything they need to know about the hotel: the location, the cost, and the amenities. The digital experience is the first touchpoint for most hotel customers, and it's an important one. *Was the information accessible? Is it easy for them to use a credit card on the website, and do they feel secure? Did an email confirmation arrive in their inbox soon after they placed the online reservation?*

2. **Contact center:** Many hotel guests have questions about their stay before they arrive at the hotel, so the next touchpoint is likely a contact center or even a person answering the phone directly at the hotel. Questions range from inquiries about valet parking to whether the hotel provides roll-away cribs and airport directions. *Was the person on the phone knowledgeable? Respectful? Friendly? Was the person able to answer customer questions?*

3. **In person:** Once guests actually arrive at the hotel, the touchpoints are almost endless. They may interact with the valet upon arrival and get help with their luggage by a bellhop. They're directed to the front desk to check in and possibly offered assistance in finding the elevator to their room. The customer might call the concierge to ask for dining recommendations, order room service, dine at restaurants within the

hotel, visit hotel spas, and exercise in the fitness center. Each of these items is a potential customer touchpoint. Checking out, either on the television in the room or at the front desk, is a key touchpoint.

4. **Post-visit:** Even after a guest checks out, the touchpoints continue when they retrieve their vehicle. After they get home, they may have questions on the final bill or call the hotel about a lost item. Of course, oftentimes the final post-visit touchpoint is asking the customer for feedback about their experience. Make sure you include this in your list!

Mapping the touchpoints for your business—in order of a typical journey, if possible—helps with prioritization of which touchpoints to focus on when measuring CX. It's not as difficult as it sounds. Simply consider how much pain a customer incurs if one of these touchpoints does not go well. I think of customer pain as a customer having such a negative experience that they decide to take their business elsewhere or provide negative feedback to other customers, publicly or privately.

The touchpoints that cause the most pain are where a business should start their VoC program! As discussed earlier, these critical touchpoints are often referred to as a *moment of truth*. These are the touchpoints where companies need feedback and where they will have to recover from and react to that feedback, if it's not positive.

Hotels often have several moments of truth in an overnight stay, but every industry has moments of truth of their own. Consider a home security company. Again, many of their customers start on a website, but then there are touchpoints that are unique to this industry—the customer may call the contact center to arrange a technician to come to their home for installation, interact with field technicians in the home for installation, and contact the accounting department once their first monthly bill arrives.

When all their touchpoints are mapped out and any previous survey feedback is considered (definitely review it if available), the customer experience team for a home security company might decide that in-home visits for customer repair are their moment of truth. This is where their transactional VoC survey should begin. When something breaks down, the team needs to know how scheduling worked for the customer, how quickly a technician resolved the problem, and whether they did, in fact, resolve the problem.

BOILING THE OCEAN

As the head of customer experience, you can run touchpoint mapping yourself. Do not feel like you need to jump right into a larger initiative called *customer journey mapping*. What I am saying is if you buy into the purpose of touchpoint mapping as identifying moments of truth in the customer experience so you can identify and prioritize your customer listening efforts, then as head of CX, you must own this.

If you make the process too complicated or involve too many people within the company, touchpoint mapping can take on a life of its own.

A typical touchpoint map should be completed in a couple of weeks, while a more detailed customer journey map can take months to complete and require a significant investment. Your job is simply to identify all the touch-points, prioritize which ones are your "moments of truth" (i.e., the touchpoints that create the most pain), and then determine how many of them can be covered inside your VoC budget, with the goal of getting customer feedback rolling in so that you can start to gain a sense for the customer's experience and drive business results.

Once you start, if you feel that you *want* to complete a full customer journey mapping exercise that determines more than just key measurement touchpoints, that's great! The initial touchpoint map provides a good foundation for a more granular customer journey map. It's important, however, that you *decide* to take this extra step rather than falling into it.

When you're working in a complex organization with

many touchpoints, the extra clarity provided from a bigger customer journey map is really helpful. These maps can help you determine how long each customer experience lasts, the individuals or teams responsible for each touchpoint, the processes and procedures involved, and how each experience should (or does) make the customer feel. CustomerBliss (www.customerbliss.com) does outstanding work in the customer journey mapping area if you are looking for help. Jeanne Bliss, the founder of CustomerBliss, has written *Chief Customer Officer*, a must-read for any CX leader. Her latest book, *Would You Do That to Your Mother?*, focuses on making business personal and is also well worth your time as a CX leader.

But the touchpoint mapping we're starting with is very focused. We are identifying where you interact with your customers, where customers could experience the most pain, and if that pain is worth measuring.

CHECKLIST FOR BUILDING A GREAT TOUCHPOINT MAP

- ☐ **Take a deep breath**; this is not as hard as it seems. You don't need to do a comprehensive customer journey map to prioritize your VoC measurement priorities.
- ☐ **Remember, you are looking to make sure you account for all of the different ways** you interact with your customers on one sheet of paper. This paper

can be a list of these interactions, or if you would like, you can create a diagram. Either way, it's fine.

☐ **The key is not how fancy** your map is; it's finding out if you have all the touchpoints accounted for and if you can prioritize these touchpoints into potential "moments of truth."

☐ **Moments of truth can be identified** by the level of pain customers could go through if this touchpoint did not go well. Typically, the real "moments of truth" are ones where you could lose a customer if not executed properly or your customer could fall in love with you if it goes well.

NOTES

IF YOU WANT A CONSISTENT EXPERIENCE ACROSS ALL TOUCHPOINTS, YOU MUST ASK FOR CUSTOMER FEEDBACK AT EACH ONE.

Once you've mapped out all your touchpoints, it's often helpful to group them into channels. There are five channels that we see often at PeopleMetrics with our clients: websites, mobile app, contact center, in location, and field services (in the home).

1. **Websites:** Refers to customers visiting websites to gather information about a company. Can include both mobile and regular versions of the website.
2. **Mobile app:** Refers to customers who download a company's app, and feedback is gathered about their experience with it.

3. **Contact center:** An important touchpoint where customers call for more information or assistance. Online chat is another part of modern contact centers.
4. **In location:** Refers to an actual in-person customer experience, such as a retail store, restaurant, or hotel.
5. **Field services:** Customers interact with a company employee in their home.

When you look at all the touchpoints on your map, each of them will likely fall into one of these five channels. No matter how your customer interacts with you, the ultimate goal is to have a consistent "omnichannel" experience. When your in-location experience is different from your web experience, or when your web experience is different from the experience a customer has with your mobile app, this inconsistent CX will create problems. Customers might feel like the company cares about them after a positive field service experience, but if the contact center fails to provide the same level of experience, the customer will be disappointed. Keep in mind that if you're working with a premium brand, all channels will need to deliver an outstanding customer experience. If you're working with a mid-tier, value-oriented brand, the goal may be to achieve a certain standard throughout each channel, such as professionalism or efficiency.

GATHERING OMNICHANNEL FEEDBACK

If you want a consistent omnichannel experience, make sure you are listening to your customers in each channel! And you can gather feedback from these five channels in various ways. For example, you might ask about their most recent experience with a field services representative through an email survey. *How satisfied were you with our technician's most recent visit to your home? Why? Were there any problems? If so, please describe them.* We are seeing more and more text surveys, or Short Message Surveys (SMS), these days as a substitute for email surveys.

Or you can gather feedback via methods that are channel specific. For website feedback, pop-up surveys can ask the customer for feedback while they are on the website or after they leave. When a customer uses a mobile app, a survey can be embedded into the app asking them to provide feedback. An interactive voice response (IVR) survey or a computer-generated survey can be used after a customer interacts with a contact center—the system directs the customer to the survey when the call is complete.

The goal is to obtain feedback from the customer in whichever way they prefer to provide you with that feedback. It will largely depend on the customer. If your primary customers are millennials, they might prefer a text message survey. If you're working with baby boomers, they probably prefer completing a survey via email at a time that's convenient for them.

CHECKLIST FOR CREATING AN OMNICHANNEL VOC PROGRAM

- ☐ **Remember that _omnichannel_ is a fancy word for being consistent** across all major customer channels—digital (website, mobile app), contact center, and in person (in location, field service).
- ☐ **Make sure the touchpoints that you mapped out** are linked to a channel so you know the most appropriate way to obtain customer feedback.
- ☐ **The only way you will know** if you are being consistent across all channels (and touchpoints) is to set up a customer feedback opportunity (sometimes called "listening posts") in each channel.
- ☐ **Some channels lend themselves to a particular method** of customer feedback—websites deliver surveys after you purchase, contact centers often offer the opportunity to provide feedback via an IVR option, and in-store experiences may include an iPad to provide feedback while the customer is in the store.
- ☐ **Remember that the goal is to enable the customer** to provide feedback the way they want that is appropriate for the given channel they are in.

NOTES

LESSON #20

DON'T FORGET THE PROSPECT EXPERIENCE IF YOU ARE B2B OR HAVE A HIGH-END B2C OFFERING.

We often think the customer experience begins when a contract is signed or when money is exchanged—after the customer is officially a customer. This simply isn't the case. The customer experience is first shaped when a customer (i.e., prospect) interacts with a member of your sales team. In the B2B world—and occasionally in the B2C world with high-priced items—the prospect's experience with the sales team is one of the most important touchpoints, and almost every business forgets to measure it. The sales team sets the expectations on what the prospect will experience once they become a customer or client. Indeed, measurable CX begins with the moment a salesperson first begins working with prospective customers.

Why do most businesses not consider the sales process as part of CX? The reason is it's not on the radar of most CX leaders who are focused on more traditional touchpoints, and most sales leaders have other priorities. It's the job of the leader of CX to insist that this key touchpoint get measured and managed.

THE CHAMPION CYCLE

At PeopleMetrics, we do regular independent research on CX topics that are important to understand and would be of value to our clients. Recently, we did independent research on the impact of the prospect experience with 800-plus B2B decision makers (called *buyers*). What we found is something we coined as the *Champion Cycle*. Here's how it works in the context of a B2B buyer purchasing something significant like SaaS software, equipment, or professional services (from companies called *providers*):

1. When purchasing something significant, B2B buyers seek out recommendations from others as their first step, almost always. In PeopleMetrics' research, we found that **78%** of B2B buyers seek recommendations from others when they're beginning a search for a new provider.

2. Next, when a provider gets a positive recommendation, it gives them a *big* advantage. Our research found that **76%** of the time, the winning provider was rec-

ommended to the B2B buyer. Not only that, losing providers were recommended only 36% of the time! In other words, if you are a provider and happen to make a B2B buyer's consideration list but you were not recommended, your chances for selection are very low.

3. The experience the B2B buyer has with the provider's sales rep during the buying process has a big impact. Our research found that **61%** of B2B buyers said the experience they had with the sales rep of the winning provider was of "high value." Losing providers did not provide this same experience as only 29% were of high value.

4. And guess what? Those sales reps delivering a high-value experience for the B2B buyer got bigger contracts! $100,000 more, in fact, compared to experiences delivered by sales reps considered to be lower value by B2B buyers.

5. The Champion Cycle is finished by this amazing finding from our research—**70%** of B2B buyers who experience high-value meetings with the sales team recommend the provider to others!

6. Rinse and repeat.

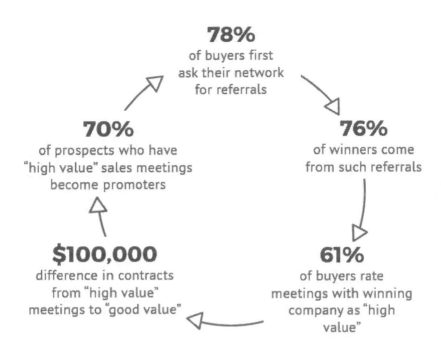

78%
of buyers first
ask their network
for referrals

76%
of winners come
from such referrals

70%
of prospects who have
"high value" sales meetings
become promoters

61%
of buyers rate
meetings with winning
company as "high
value"

$100,000
difference in contracts
from "high value"
meetings to "good value"

The bottom line is this: good salespeople tell the truth, answer questions thoroughly, and add value to the product or service they're selling. Positive buyer experiences become recommendations, which means more potential companies or customers will add your company to their consideration list.

MEASURING THE PROSPECT EXPERIENCE

PeopleMetrics has pioneered the measurement of the prospect experience via a short survey that goes out to buyers after meeting with a sales team. The survey is short, simple, and powerful! And the process is simple. Immediately after a sales call, a survey is triggered that goes to the prospect(s) whom the sales team met. Make sure you include everyone in the room, not just the decision maker or buyer. Here is what we recommend asking:

1. **Meeting value:** The first question is about how valuable the recent meeting with the sales team was—the member(s) of the sales team are always included by name in this question.
2. **Why:** This second, follow-up question gives context to how the meeting went, what value the sales team added, and any other information that the prospect wants to share.
3. **Experience:** The third question asks about specific attributes of a sales team that we found in our research to drive a great prospect experience. These include being well prepared, consultative, good listeners, knowledgeable, and proactive. (See the sidebar for definitions of each term.)
4. **Concerns:** The final question is the most important one. It simply asks, "Do you have any concerns related to moving forward in your engagement with (company)?"

That's it. The survey is always triggered after an in-person meeting, but we also recommend sending this survey out after a demo or even an initial capabilities presentation. The reason is that your company will clearly stand out from the competition (at least right now), since very few are asking for prospect feedback. But there's more. Adding the prospect experience to your VoC will enable your sales team to course-correct when the prospect experience is less than optimal. This could mean big $$$! This also lets you understand how your sales team is really performing in the eyes of prospects, and your coaching and training become much more effective. Finally, by asking if there are any issues moving forward, you can find out when there isn't a good fit early in the process before you waste time and resources.

You might be asking, "Will any prospect really fill out a survey like this?" The answer is a resounding yes! In fact, we are seeing higher response rates for our prospect experience surveys than we are with our customer experience surveys. At PeopleMetrics, our response rates for our own prospect survey is 75%. For our clients, we have seen a minimum response rate of 25% and many much higher.

Here's one more benefit of a prospect survey to keep in mind. Even if your prospect does not fill out the survey, that is telling you something! It might mean the prospect simply does not like filling out surveys, or it might mean that the last meeting your sales rep had with the prospect did not go as well as the rep thought it did. Either way, it's good reason to reach back out to the prospect to make sure.

ATTRIBUTES OF A GREAT SALES TEAM

Well prepared: Did the required preparation work for our meeting (e.g., getting up to speed on my business, delivering what was promised based on a prior meeting/conversation, etc.)

Consultative: Asked the right questions to understand my needs and shared (company) insights and point of view

Good listeners: Demonstrated good listening by going deeper to understand the issues and challenges driving my needs

Knowledgeable: Demonstrated an in-depth knowledge of (company) solutions and related them to the current needs of my organization

Proactive: Followed up in a thorough, accurate, and timely manner

CHECKLIST FOR ADDING THE PROSPECT EXPERIENCE TO YOUR VOC PROGRAM

☐ **First, determine if surveying prospects** makes sense for your industry and company. If you are B2B and are selling something of significant value (say, over $10,000), you likely have a sales team and listening to prospects makes a lot sense. Similarly, if you are B2C and selling a high-ticket item like real estate, automobiles, or insurance, surveying prospective customers is appropriate.

☐ **Next, determine when you will reach out** to prospects. After an initial meeting? After a demo? After a proposal review? All of these? I recommend the more, the better.

- [ ] **Make sure you send out the prospect experience survey as soon** after the prospect interaction as possible. This will likely require you to integrate with your CRM to make this happen (see Lesson 36).
- [ ] **Use PeopleMetrics' prospect experience survey design**: 1) meeting value, 2) why, 3) sales rep attributes, and 4) any concerns moving forward.
- [ ] **Every prospect response** should generate an alert or notification that gets sent to the sales team and the CX leader.
- [ ] **Ideally, all information gathered** in the prospect survey should be linked and updated in your CRM.

NOTES

LESSON #21

IF YOU ARE JUST STARTING OUT, START SLOW AND GET TO KNOW WHERE YOU ARE.

Here's a piece of advice that will return your investment in this book a hundred times over: If you're just starting your VoC program, *don't* begin with a transactional VoC survey right away. Start with a relationship survey instead. In the beginning of this book, I talked about a bank account that you have with every customer with all of their experiences bundled together. A relationship survey is your vehicle to understand what your balance is with each of your customers.

Why start with a relationship survey? There are three main reasons:

1. **Build your credibility quickly.** Many of your col-

leagues will not understand what you do as the head of CX. Your colleagues may know that the organization is committed to creating a great customer experience, but their understanding about *your* daily activities is often limited. Immediately surveying *all* of your company's active customers is a quick win for your VoC program. In a matter of weeks, you can show tangible data about the strength of your overall relationship with customers (via NPS typically), what you are doing really well, what you need to improve on, and how you compare to the competition. All this information allows you to demonstrate immediate value. When this happens, your role and the importance of listening to customers and improving CX are seen much more clearly. Remember, *everyone is in marketing*. You must continually show your value and the value of CX.

2. **It makes your transactional VoC survey much, much better.** Learning about the strength of the overall customer relationship, including what is making it great and what is making it painful, goes a long way toward establishing a successful VoC transactional survey. It also provides critical data on which touchpoints to begin your VoC transactional survey. For example, if you are hearing negative feedback about the contact center experience in your relationship survey, that could be a clue to start there when transitioning to a transactional VoC survey.

3. **You can get this done without involving too many**

people. You only need to really do four things to get a relationship survey done. First, make friends with IT (see Lesson 15 and obtain a list of active customers, making sure you include first name, last name, and email address at a minimum). Second, craft the relationship survey. Third, find a good survey engine or VoC partner for the program survey and send it out to your active customer list. Fourth, and most important, is analyzing the customer responses and telling a great story.

A RELATIONSHIP SURVEY STARTER

Here's a sample survey outline you can use to get started on a relationship survey.

1. NPS (How likely are you to recommend [company] to a friend or colleague?). This is based on a 0–10 scale. Refer back to NPS in Lesson 5.
   A. Why?
2. Ask respondents which touchpoints they have interacted with your company within the last *six months* (unless you know this information from your customer data file). Start with touchpoints within your major channels (in person, contact center, digital, sales). For example, a retail bank's touchpoints may include a visit to a branch, a call to the contact center, a visit to the website, logging in to the bank's mobile appli-

cation, meeting with a loan officer, and so on. This question is a check box where the respondent is able to choose more than one option.

3. Using survey logic, direct customers to appropriate touchpoint(s) so they get only questions about something they actually experienced. Map out questions related to the experience at these touchpoints. These can be up to ten questions per section. For example, continuing the earlier example, if a customer indicates they visited your bank during the past six months, you can then ask them several questions about that visit. Here are a few to consider (all based on a 5–1 agreement scale, where 5 is "strongly agree" and 1 is "strongly disagree").

   A. The branch environment is clean, bright, and inviting.

   B. The hours of operation allow me to bank on my schedule.

   C. I experience reasonable wait times.

   D. The expertise of the staff is evident in their interactions with me.

   E. Employees are friendly and attentive.

   F. My transaction is completed efficiently.

   G. I am able to achieve my goal in one visit (no follow-up or return visits needed).

Please note that you will need a battery of questions for each touchpoint that you are measuring in your relationship survey.

4. Competitive comparison. You can either have a separate section for this or include competitor comparisons in the earlier sections, but be careful; remember that each competitor you add will require the respondent to answer the full range of touchpoint questions per competitor, significantly lengthening the time to complete the survey.

5. Demographic questions.

CHECKLIST FOR STARTING YOUR VOC PROGRAM STRONG

☐ **Avoid the temptation to begin your VoC with transactional surveys** and many touchpoints.

☐ **Start slow with a relationship survey** targeting all of your active customers (usually defined as those you have done business with within the past six months).

☐ **Be prepared to offer an incentive** for your customers to complete the survey; usually a sweepstakes offering will suffice (more on incentives in Lesson 28).

☐ **A relationship survey will help you get a baseline** on where you are today (with NPS), provide an indicator as to which touchpoints are delivering positive customer experiences and which ones are not, and measure how you stack up to the competition.

☐ **Use PeopleMetrics' relationship survey starter** to create your relationship survey.

☐ **Use the results from the relationship survey to**

build your case for the importance of CX through-out your organization and to create highly effective transactional survey(s) when you are ready.

NOTES

LESSON #22

★ ★ ★ ★ ★

TRANSACTIONAL VOC SHOULD START SLOW, TOO. YOU WILL THANK ME LATER.

Now that you've taken the time to complete a relationship survey, it's time to consider continuous transactional VoC feedback. Given how transactional VoC can drive business results, the tendency is to want to go full bore into a comprehensive program. Indeed, the business benefits of transactional VoC are significant, specifically:

1. **Reducing churn:** Transactional VoC enables you to close the loop and follow up with individual customers who have problems during a recent experience and save those customers (see Lesson 30). Transactional VoC also allows you to identify what isn't working for many customers through root cause analysis (see Lesson 31) and to fix systemic problems that will pre-

vent future customer experience issues and potential churn.

2. **Increasing social reviews:** After a customer is finished with a transactional VoC survey, you are able to direct them to the social review site(s) of your choice. This provides a proactive approach to boost your social review ratings. Transactional VoC also can *prevent* a disgruntled customer from posting a negative social review by following up with the customer and fixing the issue.

3. **Increasing leads:** By including a question in your survey that asks a customer if they are interested in additional products and/or services you provide, you can generate leads for your sales team to follow up on and generate additional revenue.

So you're excited and you are ready to really make your mark by driving business results via transactional VoC, but don't get too far ahead of yourself. Again, I recommend starting slow. Best practice is to begin your transactional VoC with a pilot program. Let's consider a location-based business, like a restaurant or hotel. A pilot takes a small sample of your locations to test out transactional VoC. So if you have two hundred locations, you'll start with five or ten of them for a specified amount of time—three months often works well.

Why start with a pilot? There are three reasons:

1. **Making sure your survey makes sense:** If customers have no idea how to answer your questions, or if they don't understand the terminology you are using, they might flatline the survey (i.e., answer "3" to every question) or abandon the survey altogether. You also can test if the survey is taking customers too long to complete and if it is working on all devices/browsers.

2. **Making sure your VoC software platform works:** You can also use a pilot to create dashboards for company employees, all tied to your chosen pilot locations. You can then train the employees to log in to the dashboards, view the data, understand reports, and answer any questions. Certain data views are appropriate only for different users. An executive, for instance, may need to see just the data that shows them NPS or customer satisfaction levels, or the percentage of customers who have experienced problems. Someone responsible for a particular location, however, needs to know all of this as well as whether their front desk is effective or how their spa is doing. If you are in charge of housekeeping, you will want to know which rooms provided the highest and lowest overall guest experience ratings so that you can identify your staff's most effective housekeepers. The data that VoC provides to these operational managers must be clear and effective in meeting their needs. A pilot ensures this happens.

3. **Testing loop closing:** You can test the best ways to

follow up or "close the loop" with negative customer experiences. When there is a low NPS, or when the customer experience falls below a particular threshold, follow-up is essential. Not only is this CX best practice, but in a pilot, you also can test your follow-up process. For example, before you begin a VoC transactional survey, you won't know how many customers will have problems and whether you have the process and resources to properly follow up. In our hotel example, the location's general manager could follow up with customers who provided negative feedback—except general managers typically have a lot on their plate. This might not be a big deal if the negative feedback volume is low, but you won't know until you test the waters *before* you start your VoC program. If you ask 200 general managers to follow up with all negative customers without doing a pilot program first, you could have a big problem on your hands. Two hundred overwhelmed general managers could give up on both you and VoC before you even get started. Discuss your strategy with the pilot locations first. Reassure them that they need to follow up with customer issues, but that if there are overwhelming numbers, someone at the corporate office will help. General managers could then be responsible for contacting their location's most important customers. This gives your VoC program a greater chance at success and allows you to work out the kinks before it's rolled out.

Please note that pilots are beneficial for more than just location-based businesses. In a large company with millions of customers, start with just a handful. If there are six or seven business units, start with just one.

After a three-month pilot program, you'll have learned some important things from a select number of locations, customers, or business units. Now you'll want to take a step back and decide what worked and what didn't. Make sure your loop closers—the people who are following up on negative customer experiences—are trained and ready to go. Ask yourself which parts of your transactional VoC survey you want to apply to the entire organization. Maybe it's the questions you asked, the reports you designed for certain roles, or the customer follow-up approach. It's time to clarify, ask questions, and finalize. The pilot is the practice before the big game—the rehearsal before the performance.

A TRANSACTIONAL SURVEY STARTER

Here's a sample survey outline for a transactional VoC survey.

1. Net Promoter Score (optional)
2. Overall satisfaction with the most recent experience— this is the most important question in a transactional survey. *Do not* solely rely on NPS.

A. Why?

3. Did you experience a problem? If yes, ask: *[Follow up to reduce churn]*

    A. What general categories does the problem relate to? (This is in the form of a multiple check box question.)

    B. Please describe the problem in detail. (Open-ended)

    C. Was the problem resolved? (Yes/No)

4. Did anyone go out of their way to make your most recent experience special? If yes, ask: *[Follow up with employee recognition]*

    A. Who?

    B. What did they do?

5. The following is a full list of our products and services. Please indicate if you have interest in any of these, and we will follow up with more information. *[Follow up to generate sales leads and new revenue]*

    A. Please note this is a multiple check box item.

6. May we have permission to share your feedback and comments with others on our website and other communication vehicles? *[Include as marketing testimonials]*

    A. This is a Yes/No question.

7. If applicable, direct respondents to the social review sites of your choice. Please share your experience with: *[Follow up to reduce churn and improve social review scores]*

A. TripAdvisor

B. Yelp

C. Google Reviews

CHECKLIST FOR BUILDING A TRANSACTIONAL VOC PILOT

☐ **Choose a fraction of your locations, customers, or business units** to test out your transactional VoC program before you roll it out to the entire organization.

☐ **Your pilot could also focus on a single touchpoint** (e.g., contact center) rather than all the channels through which you reach customers (e.g., in store, in home, digital, etc.).

☐ **Make sure you are driving business results** with your VoC transactional survey. The design of your survey will allow you to reduce churn, increase social reviews, and generate new leads. You will also be able to provide employee recognition and generate marketing testimonials through a well-designed transactional VoC survey.

☐ **Once you choose the scope of your pilot** and design your survey, keep a careful eye on survey abandonment rates and the amount of time it is taking customers to fill out the survey. You may have confusing terminology, an ineffective survey invite, or simply way too many questions.

☐ **This is also the time to create and test the reports**

you will share with colleagues. Figure out the best way to train users on getting into your VoC software platform, how to best access their data, and how to create new reports and dashboards.

☐ **This time will also be invaluable to create a process for following up** with customers who had a problem or issue. You will be able to first understand what percentage of customers are likely to require such follow-up so you can plan accordingly in the full rollout. Second, you will be able to test the actual follow-up process (see more on closing loops in Lesson 30).

NOTES

SURVEY HEALTH IS EVERYTHING. THE SUCCESS OF YOUR VOC PROGRAM (AND PROBABLY YOUR JOB) DEPENDS ON IT.

At this point, you're feeling pretty good about your VoC program. You've identified key touchpoints, and a successful relationship survey has helped you figure out the best questions to include in your transactional survey. You used those questions in a pilot transactional survey and trained key users, and everyone is ready to go. However, if your transactional survey health is poor, none of that effort will matter.

Some transactional surveys have a response rate of more than 50%, but this is uncommon. A healthy transactional B2C survey will have a response rate of at least 5%; at PeopleMetrics, our range is 5% to 18% for B2C. As mentioned in the previous lesson, pilot studies help a lot with this—in fact, the likelihood of a healthy survey is much higher when you've done a pilot first. For B2B, we see response rates as high as 50%.

A good transactional VoC survey can be completed in a short amount of time. *If providing feedback takes longer than the actual customer experience, you have a major problem.* So if you're measuring a customer experience that normally lasts three minutes using a survey that takes ten minutes, it's time to go back to the drawing board. However, if a customer had a problem, response times will be increased. When there is a problem, companies need more clarity so they can figure out how to fix it, and this requires more questions. In any event, transactional VoC surveys should be no more than three to five minutes under any circumstances.

Transactional VoC surveys should also be compatible with mobile devices. The questions cannot be redundant or confusing; they should be crisp, clear, and mutually exclusive. Their answers should elicit information that you specifically need from the customer without confusing them. For example, avoid asking the customer a double-barreled question that covers two things at once: "Please tell us about your experience when you checked in and visited our restaurant."

Long-winded questions are just as confusing to customers:

"We first want to ask you about the check-in experience during your most recent stay with us. Check-in is very important to us, and we pride ourselves on a good experience. Could you please tell us, in your own words, about your check-in experience?" Customers will not even read this, let alone answer it.

Everything else—the touchpoints, the dashboards, the training, the follow-up process—depends on the health of the survey. The effort is worth it, though.

GETTING SURVEYS COMPLETED

You can craft perfect questions that look beautiful on a mobile device, but if you cannot figure out how to get a reasonable response rate (5% or more), it still won't matter. The more personalized and brand-connected your email invitation to your customers, the more it will resonate.

You might say, for example:

Hello Sally Smith,

We really appreciate your most recent stay at Hotel X on June 18. We value your feedback. The following survey should take only three minutes of your time. Thank you so much for helping us improve your experience.

Go for something short, personalized, and date-specific, including both branding and a time frame for completing the survey. Branding on this email invitation should be as specific as possible to the customer's experience with your business. For a great example of a branded and personalized survey invitation from Wyndham Vacation Ownership, please see Lesson 27.

A healthy survey also has a foolproof reminders feature. Of the completed surveys you will receive, 60% of them will be completed after your initial request to the customer, while the remaining 40% will be completed after a reminder email. Please note that the last thing you want is to send a reminder email to customers who have *already completed* your survey. Make sure your VoC software platform has the ability to send reminders only to those who have not completed the survey previously.

Put the first question of the survey directly in the invitation as well (see Lesson 27). Often, this first question gauges overall satisfaction or allows you to determine NPS (see Lesson 5). When a customer selects an answer in the message, they are taken directly to the full survey with their first question completed. This simple format adjustment bumps customer response rates from 5% to 10%. Think of it like exercising. It's difficult to start working out, but once you begin, you're more likely to finish the workout. This same principle is true for customers and surveys.

Keep in mind that when customers abandon surveys, the data they did provide is still useful. It becomes more difficult for the company to follow up because there is less context if there is a problem or a low NPS score, but as long as the customer grants permission, companies can follow up on partial surveys.

Companies that hit 50% response rates or higher follow all these guidelines for a healthy survey, plus they have strong relationships with their clients. Most of the time, this sort of return will happen in B2B. When clients feel like their feedback is an expected part of the engagement—as with accounting firms hired to audit financials or perform a highly involved technology audit—the response rates rise significantly.

CHECKLIST FOR DETERMINING SURVEY HEALTH

☐ **Make sure you have a dashboard** in your VoC software platform to allow you to easily gauge your survey health in real time, and check this regularly.

☐ **You should regularly track key survey health metrics,** such as completion rate (also called response rate), partial completion rate, completed surveys after first survey invite, completed surveys after reminder invite, average time to complete survey, and survey question abandonment triggers.

☐ **Track how many customers are being eliminated**

from receiving a survey due to "month rules" that prevent any given customer from receiving a survey invite more than once every thirty, sixty, or ninety days.

☐ **Make sure your survey is not too long** (never more than five minutes for a transactional VoC survey) and you know which questions are causing surveys to be abandoned.

☐ **Create reminder emails** (two maximum) that are sent to those customers who did not complete the survey on the initial invite.

☐ **Include the first survey question** directly in your email invitation (see Lesson 27 for a great example).

NOTES

LESSON #24

★ ★ ★ ★ ★

SHORTER SURVEYS ARE USUALLY BETTER—BUT IF IT'S TOO SHORT, IT COULD COME BACK TO BITE YOU.

The shorter your survey, the better the response rates. For that reason, super-short surveys are currently in vogue. These often have one or two questions: 1) the likelihood that the customer will recommend their company (NPS), and 2) why? Customers enjoy this type of survey because it is quick to complete. Companies like them because response rates are typically very high (30%+ for B2C, 50%+ for B2B).

But there is no free lunch, and here's the rub. A short survey will provide more responses, but those responses may not provide the granular data you need to inform your stakeholders about their CX performance levels.

Let's take a look at the hotel example that I have been using throughout this book. As a leader of CX in a hotel group with, say, one hundred locations, think about your stakeholders. There are restaurants in each location that need to know how well they're serving hotel guests, a housekeeping department that needs to know how well housekeepers are cleaning the rooms, a front desk that needs to verify that the check-in and checkout system is running smoothly, a spa that needs to understand the experience they are delivering to guests, a fitness center that requires feedback on the guest experience, and so on.

There are three major problems with asking only two questions in a transactional VoC survey:

1. **There is a lack of granularity.** With only two questions, you are essentially betting your entire VoC program on that one open-ended text box asking "Why?" after NPS. You are counting on customers to provide great detail about why their experience was good or bad, including naming specific areas of the experience that lead them to this evaluation. This anecdotal evidence that the customer provides is your only clue to explain NPS. There is no guarantee that the customer will mention the restaurant where they ate or how well the front desk did with checkout. After a quarter or so goes by and it's time to deliver results to the team, you'll most likely come up short.

This leaves you, the head of CX, basically making an educated guess about how well company stakeholders performed based on very little information. This doesn't make stakeholders happy. Trust me on this. They will question. They will poke holes. They won't accept things easily. They're going to ask how you arrived at your conclusions, and they're going to want to see "their" data. Ultimately, a survey that is too short can derail a VoC program.

2. **NPS does not measure the most recent customer experience.** The NPS question is used on transactional VoC surveys all the time. The issue with relying on NPS only is that it fails to measure the customer's latest experience. As I have mentioned many times in this book, NPS is a measure of the overall relationship you have with your customer; it does not tell you how well you just did with that customer during their last interaction.

3. **Are you willing to bet your job on text analytics?** Even if you're willing to accept the first two issues, you better have a really, really good text analytics program (see Lesson 4) to make sense out of the open-ended comments. If you have 10,000 open-ended survey responses coming in daily, you cannot review each one without the use of text analytics. Your text analytics algorithm must then be made extremely precise for you to receive accurate data, because you're relying on it big time!

I totally get why super-short surveys are an attractive option. You want high response rates because that makes a healthier survey, and two questions seems like a much better experience for the customer than ten or twenty questions. But your job, as the VoC leader, is an interdisciplinary one. You have to consider external *and* internal customers alike. You must be able to deliver operational CX feedback to your stakeholders, or you are toast.

It's a tricky balance between the extremes. Too long, and a survey will not be healthy and may produce only negative feedback, if any at all. Too short, and even completed surveys will not produce helpful information. The decisions you make about how many questions to ask, when you're going to ask them, and how often you're going to ask them will determine how effective you are in your role.

If two questions are too short for your transactional survey, and thirty questions are too long, where's the sweet spot? Shoot for a transactional survey that has between eight and fifteen simple-to-answer questions that take customers no more than five minutes total to complete. An outline of such a transactional VoC survey is provided in Lesson 22.

IDEAL SURVEY LENGTH VARIES

In larger companies, VoC results are important to many

groups, and leaders are often held accountable for certain scores. Their jobs are evaluated, at least partially, on the customer experience that their teams deliver.

If many of your stakeholders are evaluated on their ability to deliver a good customer experience and incentive compensation works into their evaluation—their bonus or continued employment rides on customer feedback—a two-question survey is probably not enough. Feedback should be objective and consistent. With no objective measure on their performance, your stakeholders become skeptical of the VoC program. And why shouldn't they? Their income rides on your program's results.

In a smaller enterprise, a two-question survey might work. Small businesses without as many stakeholders can benefit from a survey this short, especially when they simply need regular customer feedback. But if you must have a really short survey and insist on NPS as one of the questions, please add a question that gauges the overall satisfaction with the most recent experience. That way, you get both NPS scores that executives love plus operational information about the latest experience. I would also recommend using the open-ended question (i.e., "Why?") after the customer satisfaction question so you can understand the context behind why recent customer experiences were positive or negative. So that's a total of three questions: NPS, CSAT, and "Why?"

CHECKLIST FOR BUILDING A TRANSACTIONAL VOC SURVEY THAT IS THE RIGHT LENGTH

☐ **If you are an enterprise with multiple stakeholders** who care about CX or whose jobs are evaluated based on how well they deliver CX, don't use a two-question survey!

☐ **Remember, your job is to provide customer feedback** that your operating colleagues can use to understand how well they are delivering an experience. A two-question survey will severely hinder your ability to do this.

☐ **Your survey should be long enough to get operational data** to your stakeholders, but not a question longer. For transactional VoC, this usually means a minimum of eight questions. Many of PeopleMetrics' clients have fifteen to twenty questions.

☐ **It is key to make sure your questions will capture** the operational CX data you need to deliver to your stakeholders.

☐ **A two-question survey will also limit the business impact** of your VoC program. Your ability to reduce churn is limited to following up on the NPS question only (i.e., no information on a specific problem that occurred recently), and there is no chance to generate leads for additional business or recognize employees who delivered a special experience because these questions are not asked.

☐ **You really don't need to use NPS in transactional**

VoC surveys; this is a measure of the customer relationship. It tells you little about how the most recent customer experience went. However, if your executive team requires regular reporting of NPS, then by all means include it in your transactional VoC.

☐ **If you are a small enterprise** without many stakeholders or want to use a short survey, add a question that gauges how well the most customer recent experience went. This can be a simple customer satisfaction question or customer effort question (see Lesson 6).

NOTES

LESSON #25

★ ★ ★ ★ ★

CUSTOMER SAMPLE LISTS ARE THE MOST CHALLENGING PART OF ANY VOC PROGRAM.

At this point, we've discussed a lot about VoC surveys, including the different surveys you can select (relationship, transactional) and the channels you can deliver these surveys in (digital, contact center, in person). We know where we should begin with moments of truth where the customer feels the most pain, the preferred length of surveys, and how we make our surveys healthy and strong. But even if we do all of these things, the feedback will *still* not be helpful if your customer lists are not right or you cannot get them at all.

Customer lists are often called *sample lists*, and they are the primary bottleneck that will prevent you from listening to customers on a regular basis. As I mentioned in Lesson

15, making friends with IT will help you get a regular list of customers who had a recent transaction. This is key to *everything* regarding the initial success of your VoC program. When you decide to distribute a relationship survey, for example, you'll need IT to help you identify all active customers. You need at least their full name and their email address to contact them. Relationship survey customer lists are relatively easy, which is why I talked about the benefits of starting here in Lesson 21.

A transactional VoC survey is where things can get complicated. The reason is you don't just need a snapshot of active customers. You need a regular feed of transactional customer information—in other words, customers who have had an interaction with your company via some channel within some very recent time period. Where is this information? It depends. It could be in your CRM, in a financial system, or in a point-of-sale system. As we discussed in Lesson 15, the IT department should quickly become your best friend. They're often the best people to talk to about obtaining customer lists. Please note that not only do you need all of their contact information, but you also need to know when the customers had their last transaction with the company.

The key part of an effective VoC program is distributing the survey as quickly after a transaction date as possible. But this is easier said than done. However, it is possible to anticipate this hurdle and plan ahead—even before you write your first question in your survey. After you select your first touchpoint, it's time to brainstorm how you're going to collect the customer lists required to get regular feedback. If your touchpoint is the company's contact center, a customer list should include the customer first/last name, the customer email address, when the customer called, the agent who handled the call, and the length of the call. You'll need to determine how to get the information out of your internal systems so it can be transferred to your VoC software platform.

You'll also need to figure out how you'll automate this process. Rather than receiving a flat file in CSV or Excel format every day from IT, use APIs to automate this key task. A good VoC software provider will help you figure this out for sure and should be able to provide their own APIs that can communicate with your internal systems to make things easier for everyone.

Where your data lives will be determined by the touchpoint you choose to measure. Let's say that you're focusing on the prospect experience with your sales team (B2B). Where might you find this information? Most likely, it's located in your CRM. CRMs track all sales activity—from the time the salesperson introduces a product or service to a prospect and designs a proposal to when the deal is closed. Reach out to the department that manages your

CRM to gain access when prospects and salespeople interact. You'll send out your survey soon after that interaction.

No matter the touchpoint, email surveys are still the most prevalent type of survey, so having a continually updated customer email list is crucial for your VoC program and other company initiatives. SMS or text surveys are becoming more popular too, especially in the telecommunications industry. Companies like AT&T and Verizon can send you a text message with a link to the survey free of charge because they are providing the wireless service and your phone number. In any case, setting up a process where both email addresses and mobile phone numbers are continually updated will provide you with what you need to make your VoC world class!

CHECKLIST FOR REDUCING THE CUSTOMER LIST BOTTLENECK

- ☐ **Make friends with IT.** Take key members out to dinner; buy them gifts; do whatever you have to do. They are probably the ones who can help you get access to the customer data you need for your VoC to work.
- ☐ **At a minimum, if you are sending out an email survey**, your list will need to include first name, last name, email address, the date/time of interaction, and interaction type (phone call, visit to store, etc.).

Ideally, this also includes the name of the employee whom the customer interacted with during their experience (if applicable).

☐ **For a relationship survey,** ask IT for a one-time customer list based on active customers (those who have interacted with your company within the past six to twelve months). This is relatively straightforward.

☐ **For a transactional survey,** push for an automated feed from your internal system (CRM, point-of-sale) to your VoC software provider's system. This will make your life a lot easier!

☐ **If you can't get your customer list automated** immediately, obtain CSV files that contain key customer information, and upload them to your VoC software provider's system. This is a short-term fix and is not recommended for the long run.

NOTES

LESSON #26

★ ★ ★ ★ ★

CHEAP, GENERIC SURVEYS SAY A LOT ABOUT HOW YOU FEEL ABOUT YOUR CUSTOMERS (AND IT'S NOT GOOD).

A company that's investing in VoC clearly cares about the customer experience. However, the manner in which you ask customers for their feedback is just as important as the experience itself. If you use a cheap, generic survey tool to ask for feedback, customers know. When you distribute a survey that lacks branding and customization, you're basically telling them that you don't care *that* much about their experience. Cheap DIY survey tools are fine for PTAs and local swimming clubs, but a professional VoC program should think twice before using them.

At PeopleMetrics, we tested the customer perception of a branded, customized email invitation versus a generic email invitation. The first featured the client's logo and colors with an attractive font, a short message, and an executive's handwritten digital signature (see an example in Lesson 23). The second was similar to a generic survey invitation you'd see from a typical survey tool. The branded, signed letter had double the response rate compared to the generic email invitation.

Don't get me wrong—DIY survey tools are a great option if you want to know what your neighbors think about Little League uniforms or where your employees would like the next holiday party to take place. But VoC is not Little League. It's a systematic, operational program to collect, understand, and take action on customer feedback so that you can improve the customer experience and drive business results. You need more than a survey tool to accomplish this. You need a professional VoC software platform that makes your external and internal customers feel like you really care about CX.

Remember, it's as important to deliver a great customer experience when you are *asking* for feedback as when you *interacted* with the customer in the first place! The is part of an omnichannel experience. All the money and time spent on creating a superb customer experience during your primary interaction is wasted if you treat the feedback component like a bargain basement afterthought.

CHECKLIST FOR DELIVERING A GREAT EXPERIENCE AT THE FEEDBACK TOUCHPOINT

☐ **When doing your touchpoint map** (see Lesson 18), make sure you include customer feedback as a touchpoint.

☐ **Remember, just like with other touchpoints,** the way you make the customer feel when they provide feedback is influenced by how much they perceive you care about them.

☐ **Using a professional VoC software provider** will enable you to provide a great experience for both your customers who are providing feedback and your colleagues who are acting on this feedback.

☐ **Make sure your email invitation is branded** and professional, includes details about the experience, renders on all devices, and includes the first question directly in the invite (see Lesson 27).

☐ **Most DIY survey tools,** while incredibly useful for local groups like PTAs, are not designed for collecting continuous customer feedback across multiple touchpoints with many stakeholders needing to view and act on their data. Going in this direction is penny wise and pound foolish.

☐ **Most DIY survey tools lack advanced VoC features** that you will need, such as text analytics, advanced alert management, root cause analysis, and branded email invites for multiple brands/locations.

NOTES

LESSON #27

PUT THE FIRST SURVEY QUESTION IN THE EMAIL INVITATION—ALWAYS.

Here is a practical lesson that, if you follow it, will immediately pay dividends in terms of increased response rates and a healthier survey. Put your first survey question directly in your email invitation. If you're not doing this already, it's an easy change to make. I can't think of a reason why you shouldn't do this. Make this change, and response rates will rise from 5% to 10% immediately. I've included an example in a Wyndham Vacation Ownership survey.

From: Wyndham Vacation Resorts <WVO@peoplemetrics.com>
Sent: Friday, March 2, 2018 1:05 PM
To: McDade, Sean <sean.mcdade@peoplemetrics.com>
Subject: Your recent stay at Wyndham Bonnet Creek Resort

Thank you!

Dear Sean,

We're committed to making every stay an exceptional one, so we'd love to hear about your recent stay at Wyndham Bonnet Creek Resort.
Our short survey will take you just a few minutes to complete and will help us make sure every experience you have with us is a memorable one.

To begin the survey, please respond to the following question:
How likely is it that you would recommend Wyndham to a friend?

Extremely Likely										Not at all Likely
10	9	8	7	6	5	4	3	2	1	0
○	○	○	○	○	○	○	○	○	○	○

Alternatively, you may use this link to begin the survey: https://survey.peoplemetrics.com/es/76E1C0635A53D034

Thanks for staying with us at Wyndham Bonnet Creek Resort, we look forward to welcoming you back again soon. Happy Vacationing!

Sincerely,
Ken Kozielski
Vice President, Customer Experience
Wyndham Vacation Ownership

You will also notice that Wyndham Vacation Ownership followed other survey health best practices noted in Lesson 23, including a personalized message from Ken Kozielski, Vice President of Customer Experience, referencing the specific property within their network where I stayed (Bonnet Creek) and including Wyndham Vacation Ownership branding directly in the email invite.

Surprisingly, many survey invitations still contain only a long link to the survey. When customers click that link, they're sometimes directed to another page with text describing the survey before they're redirected—yet again—to the first question. By this point, some customers drop off, stopping the survey without providing feedback.

An email invitation with the first question embedded like the earlier Wyndham Vacation Ownership example will launch the customer into the survey without them even realizing it! Being able to answer the first question directly in the email invitation will provide the momentum they'll need to finish. With higher response rates and more feedback, you'll have more data for stakeholders and more opportunities to follow up with unhappy customers.

Your first question should be quantitative, asking about either the most recent experience or NPS. These days, the standard first question is often NPS as in the earlier example. The second most common embedded first question asks customers about their overall satisfaction with the most recent experience.

Please note, when customers "answer" this first question in the email, it's technically not recorded directly in the email invitation; rather, the answer you select is saved and you are taken to the actual survey. Here is an example of me responding to the NPS question that was included in the Wyndham Vacation Ownership email invitation shown previously.

WYNDHAM
VACATION OWNERSHIP®

Technical questions or problems? We are here to help!

1. How likely is it that you would RECOMMEND WYNDHAM to a friend?

Extremely Likely										Not at all Likely
10	9	8	7	6	5	4	3	2	1	0
○	●	○	○	○	○	○	○	○	○	○

Next

My answer of "9" triggered the NPS screen. It saved that answer, and when I clicked on "Next," it took me to the next question in the survey, asking me to rate my overall experience.

WYNDHAM
VACATION OWNERSHIP®

Technical questions or problems? We are here to help!

2. Please rate your OVERALL RESORT EXPERIENCE with your stay at PROPERTY.

Delighted!				Disappointed!
●	○	○	○	○

Previous   Next

And we are off to the races! As an aside, also notice how Wyndham Vacation Ownership is applying more best practices by following NPS with a question about the overall experience at my recent visit to their beautiful Bonnet Creek Resort in Orlando.

One word of caution: your first question in your email *must* be a quantitative question or one where there are radio buttons for choices. It's never a good idea to ask for qualitative feedback in the first question in the survey. Plus, there are major technological hurdles to make this happen anyway.

Think of it as going to the gym and starting with a 400-pound bench press. Most people like to warm up first by hopping on the treadmill or stretching. This first embedded question is a warm-up for the customer.

Customers do not start their day thinking about providing feedback to you via a survey, just like most people don't like to go to the gym. But once they get to the gym and start working out, they normally finish what they're doing. It's the same idea with the survey. Including the first question in your email invitation will get your customer warmed up, and they are much more likely to finish the survey and provide valuable feedback.

CHECKLIST FOR INCLUDING THE FIRST SURVEY QUESTION IN YOUR EMAIL INVITATION

- ☐ **Trust me, do this.**
- ☐ **Make sure it is a quantitative question**—either NPS or a question about their most recent experience. This should *not* be an open-ended question.
- ☐ **See the first item** on this checklist.

NOTES

LESSON #28

TO INCENTIVIZE OR NOT TO INCENTIVIZE—THAT IS THE QUESTION.

Incentives for customers to answer questions from companies come from the market research world, where long surveys are common and incentives are necessary. Physicians might be asked to complete extremely technical market research surveys about the medications they prescribe and their perceptions of various options. A survey like this can take up to an hour to complete, and physicians require hundreds of dollars to take time out of their day to participate. This is not the kind of survey that we're talking about. Very few transactional VoC surveys provide an incentive to every customer who participates. You will go broke doing this, given the continuous nature of transactional VoC.

When incentives are offered for longer relationship surveys and even some transactional surveys, it's typically in the form of a sweepstakes or drawing. There are, however, strict guidelines for these types of incentives, and the size of the prize matters. In a relationship survey, you might see an incentive for a chance to win an Amazon gift card valued at $250. A transactional survey might offer a monthly drawing for an iPad mini worth $400.

Whatever the incentive, the key is for it to be valued less than $500. More than $500, and the company must report it to the IRS as income for the recipient. With this kind of red tape, why offer incentives in the first place? Because incentives bump up your response rate by as much as 10% for a meaningful prize.

Transactional VoC surveys lend themselves to a particular type of incentive, usually a company product that is worth giving to all customers in exchange for their feedback. For example, restaurants might offer a free dessert the next time the customer visits. This incentive not only thanks them for their business but also provides a reason to return in the future. You'll see this technique used at hotels with a percentage off the customer's next spa visit or a free appetizer at the hotel restaurant. In the long run, this kind of incentive pays off with more survey responses and more return visits.

There's also a psychological component to incentives.

People like to feel like their odds to win are favorable, so it's better to offer three prizes at $150 each than it is to offer one prize worth $450. The more prizes, the better, as long as the prizes are meaningful. Giving away dollar bills to 499 people would be a worthless incentive, since the chance to win $1 won't motivate most people to act. People become interested when you are in the $50 to $100 range.

It's better to choose a safe prize that won't jeopardize your business than it is to have a creative prize that turns off your audience. If the prize is not appropriate for the audience, customers feel like the incentive is a gimmick. When they consider the prize meaningless, frivolous, or offensive, both the brand and the customer experience are impacted. An alcoholic drink coupon may sound like an ideal giveaway, but a dessert or appetizer is probably a safer, smarter choice that appeals to everyone.

A/B TESTING

If an incentive doesn't lead to more completed surveys, you will be spending money unnecessarily. How can you tell whether your incentive will deliver ROI? The answer is an A/B test. This is done by splitting your customers in half—one group has an incentive, the other does not. After you receive a minimum of, say, 200 responses from each group, you can determine whether the incentive made a difference. A significant difference in survey responses for the incentive group compared to the non-incentive group tells you that the investment in incentives might be worthwhile. *Might* is still the key word, though. If your incentive costs are high, you have to do the math to make sure the response rate or the business results generated for obtaining more customer feedback are enough to warrant the increased investment in incentives.

An A/B test becomes an A/B/C test when you test no incentive, three Amazon gift cards at $100 each, and two gift cards at $150. You can also test the response rate for a dessert coupon versus an appetizer coupon or a spa discount versus a food credit. The possibilities are endless with the concept of A/B testing. For example, you can play with the subject line on your email invitation to see which subject line yields the highest response rate between "Thank you for staying with us. We value your feedback," and "Your voice is important to us." Incentives can even be teased in subject lines as well, allowing you to test whether that makes a difference in the number of survey responses you receive. Test A might say, "Earn a chance to win $250 by providing your feedback," while Test B simply asks the customer for their feedback. When you have the right subject line, the right incentive, and the right invitation, A/B testing is an amazing way to optimize your VoC program.

One final word: it's easy to lose focus and keep testing,

but continuous testing is unnecessary once your key elements are in place. A/B tests are useful in the beginning of your VoC program while you're in the Building Phase and running pilots. Test subject lines, incentives, and email copy to thoroughly optimize your program. By the time you officially roll out your transactional VoC survey, you will be confident that the optimal elements are in place.

CHECKLIST FOR USING INCENTIVES WISELY TO BOOST YOUR RESPONSE RATE

- [ ] **Incentives are a great way to boost response** rates in your VoC program, but use them wisely.
- [ ] **For most VoC programs, both relationship and transactional surveys use a sweepstakes** incentive approach where a handful of customers who complete the survey receive a meaningful prize such as an iPad, Bose headphones, or simply an Amazon gift card worth $50 or more.
- [ ] **To optimize your incentive,** try A/B testing whereby you break out your customers into two or more groups. Offer one group an incentive and another group no incentive. See how many more completed surveys you get (if any) by offering an incentive. Make sure the differences are statistically significant. Also make sure you are selecting your groups via random sampling so every customer has an equal chance of being in Group A or Group B.

- ☐ **If you find an incentive works overall,** then try A/B testing with various incentive types and amounts. See if Amazon gift cards work better than iPads, or if four $100 prizes yield more completed surveys than one $400 prize.
- ☐ **If appropriate, consider using your own products** as incentives. For example, offer a free dessert to every customer (no sweepstakes). This is not costing you much to provide, and you will more than make it up by the revenue generated by the customer's return visit.
- ☐ **A/B testing can be used to optimize** more than incentives; consider using the technique on your subject line to your email invitation, the actual message in your invite, or even your survey questions. Keep in mind that you can optimize forever and there are diminishing returns.
- ☐ **Don't include an incentive of more than $499, or you will need to report it the IRS.**

NOTES

LESSON #29

SOCIAL REVIEWS ARE YOUR MOST IMPORTANT SURVEYS—BECAUSE THEY ARE PUBLIC SURVEYS!

Here's a fact: your most important survey comes in the form of unsolicited feedback that is posted to social media for the world to see. This lesson is largely for B2C companies that are in industries where customers are inclined to provide feedback on social review sites like TripAdvisor, Yelp, Google Reviews, Facebook, etc.

B2B interactions are not captured in social reviews because there simply is not enough volume. For example, no small business is going to post a public review about their accountant, and American Airlines is not going to post about their interactions with Boeing.

If you are in a B2B business, you can skip to the next lesson (unless you are curious).

Until now, the surveys we've discussed have been private—meaning you solicited the feedback from customers via a survey invitation of some kind. Your intention is not to share the results with the world, except maybe adding a positive customer testimonial to marketing materials (see Lesson 30). Negative customer feedback is for internal use only—not public display. But social media does not discriminate.

Hotel visits provide a classic example of the power of social reviews. Once a guest completes their stay (or even during their stay, as is more and more common), they can go to TripAdvisor and provide a rating for their overall experience in the form of stars, one to five. TripAdvisor will also prompt them to share their perceptions of value, facilities, and the check-in process, and customers can provide detailed explanations of their ratings. Thousands of people read these reviews, and for categories like hotels and restaurants, as well as product sites like Amazon, reviews can have major influence.

MANAGING SOCIAL REVIEWS

If your customers are providing social reviews, you *must* manage this feedback. But what does managing social reviews mean?

It means actively and consistently following up on each and every social review. It means that someone in your organization is responsible for responding to social reviews and thanking customers for their feedback, good or bad. Someone should directly reach out to each customer who had a bad customer experience so they know that your company truly cares. Positive reviews should be celebrated and reinforced publicly; negative reviews should be addressed with a genuine apology and assurance that steps are being taken to improve.

In most social reviews, the identity of the customer is not revealed, so companies must rely on reviewers to follow up with them after this initial outreach. How do you get in touch with a customer who provides a negative review when you don't know who they are? First, acknowledge that you understand the issue and apologize to the customer on the site where they provided the negative review. Indicate how the problem will be remedied, then provide your name, phone number, and email address to the customer so they can *contact you*. More than 50% of the time, customers will respond to you and discuss the problem.

As mentioned previously, because of the personal relationship that B2B clients have with employees at the B2B organization, they are often reluctant to publicly air their grievances. They'd rather speak with their contacts at the company directly or simply stop doing business with the company altogether when a problem arises. It's unlikely that a B2C customer knows the person selling them their phone, answering their phone call, or checking them in at a hotel. Without that personal relationship, B2C customers are more comfortable airing their concerns in a public forum.

USING VOC TO OPTIMIZE SOCIAL REVIEWS

Social reviews are arguably more important than surveys, because they're public and because many potential customers use them to decide on future purchases. You must manage these directly as described earlier; they are your most important survey. However, the best way to manage negative social reviews is *preventing them in the first place!*

VoC programs serve as insurance for companies greatly impacted by social reviews. For example, many of PeopleMetrics' restaurant clients are extremely proactive in using their VoC survey program to prevent negative social reviews. Here's how it works. After each meal, the server provides the diner with the check and an iPad they can use to provide feedback if they choose. When diners submit negative feedback, the restaurant general manager is alerted immediately about a problem. They then can remedy the situation before the customer returns home and posts a negative Yelp or OpenTable review!

This process works the same in the hospitality industry. For example, hotels can send surveys to guests twenty-four hours after check-in to circumvent negative social reviews from guests during their stay. If a guest responds with negative feedback to the survey during their stay, the hotel general manager can address the problem with the guest before they check out and before they provide a negative review on TripAdvisor! Guests should still receive a longer transactional survey after they check out, which will also help circumvent negative social reviews.

Besides providing insurance against negative social reviews, VoC programs also allow customers to easily provide a social review after completing their transactional survey, as was shown in Lesson 22.

Nine times out of ten, companies that are focused on the customer experience will deliver a great experience and receive positive reviews. The goal and challenge with social reviews is getting those nine happy customers to share their feedback on social review sites. The one unhappy customer usually finds their way to the site by themselves. By using a system to push more customers to complete social reviews, you facilitate the positive reviews. VoC programs make this happen.

DEALING WITH TWITTER AND OTHER SOCIAL NOISE

The other kind of social feedback—from social media sites like Twitter—has to be considered as well. With structured social review sites, customers are asked to rate their experience from one to five stars, and they're given the opportunity to specifically share what the experience was like. With generic social media sites, people can post any random thought they want, with no rating or consistency attached. These are the "United is horrible" or the "My experience with Delta had to be seen to be believed" comments you see on social media.

If the company is big enough, you might have a social media team separate from the customer experience group that constantly monitors these social media sites and can respond to customers quickly in a similar manner described previously in this lesson. You'll usually see a team like this in a very large company that has enough resources and manpower to devote time to responding to social chatter. This data is very hard to analyze, so someone has to decide, on a case-by-case basis, whether they are going to follow up with a customer.

As the head of CX, it's not worth your time or money to respond to general social media feedback. Let the marketing or reputation management department take on the random tweets and angry Facebook posts. You and your team should be laser-focused on customer feedback that is solicited through your VoC survey program and unsolicited through known social review sites.

CHECKLIST FOR MANAGING SOCIAL REVIEWS

☐ **When a customer provides a negative social review** on a public site like TripAdvisor, this is your most important survey and you must respond swiftly and appropriately.

☐ **Your response to a negative social review is also public,** so make sure you acknowledge that you understand the issue, be sympathetic, and offer an authentic apology.

☐ **Unlike solicited surveys where you know the name** and contact information of the customer who provided negative feedback, social reviews are anonymous, so you will need to offer your contact information and ask the customer to get in touch with you. Make sure you provide your full name and multiple ways to contact you (email, text, phone).

☐ **When you speak to the customer, make sure you get to the bottom** of what happened and do your best to resolve the situation. Offering a discount or free item is often a great way to win the customer back. Encourage the customer to come back and post a positive social review if the experience was up to expectations.

- [ ] **You should respond to positive social reviews as well.** This is a way to toot your own horn a bit and celebrate success (and encourage new customers to try you out!)
- [ ] **Your solicited VoC survey program is a great way to prevent negative social reviews** from happening in the first place! By knowing that a negative experience happened and following up immediately, the customer is much less likely to post a negative social review.
- [ ] **Solicited surveys are also a great way to increase your chances of more positive social reviews** being posted. Simply offer your customer an option at the end of your survey to link to a social review site like TripAdvisor and post a review. If you are delivering a great customer experience most of the time, this will result in far more positive social reviews.
- [ ] **Ensure your VoC software platform can compile both social review and survey data** into one system so you can easily compare the sentiment from unsolicited and solicited customer feedback.

NOTES

SECTION FIVE

OPERATIONALIZING VOC

LESSON #30

★ ★ ★ ★ ★

CLOSING THE LOOP ON ALERTS PROVIDES IMMEDIATE ROI. GET THEM RIGHT!

I have mentioned the term "closing the loop" several times in the book so far. You should get familiar with it and how important it is to VoC. With transactional VoC, when an individual customer has a problem, the front line of the operation is notified about it and can follow up to make things right. In other words, operators are able to "close the loop" with the customer, resolve any issues, and reduce the chance of churn.

Closing the loop may not sound like a big deal, but fifteen years ago, when CX measurement was owned by market research, this kind of individual customer feedback was not reported on. It wasn't shared with the employees who could respond to the feedback and resolve issues.

Today, customer-facing teams know when a customer has a problem, and they're able to use workflows in their VoC software platform to close the loop. The ability to follow up and resolve customer issues immediately is reason alone to invest in VoC. And indeed, this is why many companies do and you should too.

In its most basic form, closing the loop means that your VoC software platform "alerts" people within the organization when something happened (usually something negative) during the last customer experience. These alerts or notifications summarize the issue and often provide suggestions about what should be done next.

Alerts are integral to VoC. They let the company know about problems in real time and why they're occurring, and most importantly, they allow employees to follow up directly with the customer. With real human conversations happening between the company and the customer, issues can be resolved. That might look like anything from a sincere apology to a discount or full refund.

Believe it or not, even these days many businesses do nothing when a customer indicates there is an issue! So if you commit to closing the loop with customers, you will differentiate your company in the marketplace.

In my experience, loop closing makes transactional VoC

the *anti*-market research. When I first started in this business, PeopleMetrics was one of the first companies to issue alerts based on individual customer experiences. The market research community did not get it or like it. Our clients, however, loved it. They started to see value in VoC—not only once or twice a year, but every single day.

TYPES OF ALERTS

There are three main types of alerts that we use at PeopleMetrics in transactional VoC: *recover alerts*, *recognize alerts*, and *grow alerts*.

Recover alerts are triggered when a customer is considered *at risk* of leaving the company or sharing a negative experience on a social review site. These are also sometimes called *service recovery alerts*, *problem alerts*, *at-risk customer alerts*, or simply *real-time alerts*. These are all the same thing and indicate that you need to follow up with the customer.

What are some common instances that trigger a recover alert? When field service representatives do not show up at a house when they said they'd be there, when a contact center representative fails to resolve a customer issue in the expected time frame, when staff members are rude to customers, when food is served cold, when a room is dirty when guests check in, and many more. It's really anything that would cause a customer to indicate at least one of these on a transactional VoC survey: 1) NPS below 7 (i.e., a detractor), 2) poor overall customer experience on a recent visit, or 3) that a problem occurred during their most recent experience. Most of our clients set up multiple triggers for recover alerts so that if any of the preceding events happen, they know about it and can assign someone to follow up and close the loop with the customer.

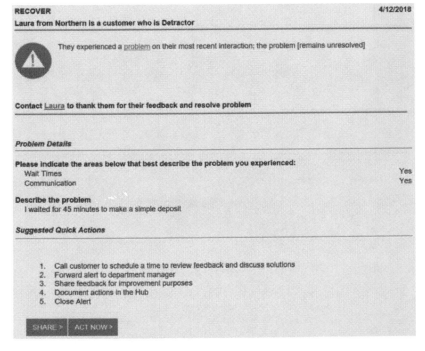

Recognize alerts are triggered when a customer indicates that they had an exceptional experience when interacting with an employee during a recent experience. These are also sometimes called *kudos alerts* or *high five alerts*. Maybe an employee goes out of their way to assist a customer or goes above and beyond to make the customer experience a positive one. *An important point is that most alerts triggered at PeopleMetrics—up to 70% for some clients—are recognize alerts.*

A recognize alert is triggered by a single question: "Did anyone go out of their way to provide an exceptional experience in your most recent visit with us?" If the customer answers, "Yes," the recognize alert is triggered. You should also ask the customer if they remember the employee's name (or include this in a list for the customer to choose from) and what the employee did to make the customer feel special.

Recognize alerts should always also go to the manager of the person who delivered an exceptional experience. Typically, this alert will then be forwarded to the employee with a congratulatory and appreciative message. That is what most companies do in terms of following up or "closing the loop" with regard to recognize alerts.

They experienced above and beyond service from these employees: Janine

Contact Diana to thank them for their feedback

Above and Beyond Service Details

Please provide the name of the banking associate(s) who provided above and beyond service. ABC Bank will personally follow up to share your feedback.
Janine

Please describe what the banking associate(s) did to go above and beyond
Getting a new loan for my business was very confusing, but Janine was very knowledgeable and really helped me understand all the steps along the way.

Suggested Quick Actions

1. Forward Alert to Janine
2. Include a Personal Thank You
3. Consider copying others
4. Share in group meeting
5. Document actions in the Hub
6. Close Alert

SHARE >   ACT NOW >

Grow alerts (also called *upsell alerts*) are triggered when a customer indicates that they are interested in additional products and services from a company. These alerts are turned into leads to be managed by the sales team. Sometimes, grow alerts are also triggered by a customer who is willing to provide specific referrals to other customers who might be a good fit for the company's products or services. Often, grow alerts can be more valuable for a company than recognize or even recover alerts.

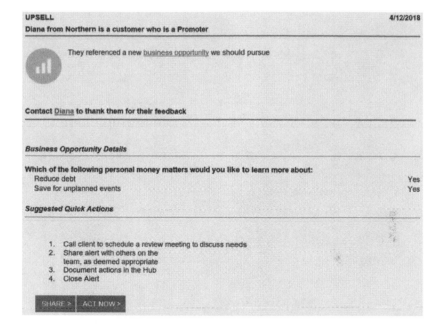

UPSELL 4/12/2018
Diana from Northern is a customer who is a Promoter

They referenced a new business opportunity we should pursue

Contact Diana to thank them for their feedback

Business Opportunity Details

Which of the following personal money matters would you like to learn more about:
Reduce debt Yes
Save for unplanned events Yes

Suggested Quick Actions

1. Call client to schedule a review meeting to discuss needs
2. Share alert with others on the team, as deemed appropriate
3. Document actions in the Hub
4. Close Alert

SHARE > ACT NOW >

RESPONDING TO RECOVER ALERTS

For B2C companies with large numbers of customers, recover alert follow-up should be prioritized by the customer's customer lifetime value (CLV). Start with the customers who have the highest CLV, then proceed from there. For B2B companies, every recover alert should include a follow-up—no exceptions!

Let's talk about the two primary strategies companies use to respond to recover alerts.

The first is a *centralized model*. It's best for organizations with a large volume of alerts. In this model, a centralized team is composed of a handful of members who are responsible for closing the loop on all recover alerts. If they cannot resolve the issue themselves, they often assign the case to someone in the organization who can. But they are always involved in the process and are ultimately responsible for closing out all recover alerts.

For organizations with fewer alerts or with a high-touch business model, a *decentralized model* often works best. In this model, alerts go directly to the location or department where the issue began. In a high-end hotel, for instance, alerts often go directly to a location's general manager. There's no need for a centralized team to decide whether they follow up or forward the alert. This individual at the hotel where the alert was based will either follow up themselves or assign the alert to someone at the hotel who is better equipped to resolve it. For example, a recover alert about a dirty hotel room may go to the leader of housekeeping.

There is a trade-off with the centralized and decentralized models. In a centralized model, you have to hire people, which adds to overall costs. But in a decentralized approach, you're adding more responsibility to the company's general managers and department heads whose job is to deliver a great customer experience. Even if they're reassigning the alerts, they still have to filter through them. This can be a major daily undertaking when a lot of alerts are involved.

Recover alerts also require the most attention when it comes to setting up a process to consistently follow up and close the loop. The first step is to identify the appropriate person to follow up with the customer and make sure they do so as soon as possible! Timing is everything when you're dealing with unhappy customers, regardless of your industry, but for some industries, the stakes are higher. For example, restaurants and hotels risk customers posting on social media and review sites during or immediately after their experience. If a hotel guest provides feedback on Monday morning at 10:00 a.m., following up with them that afternoon is much better than if you wait a week. As a general rule, companies should *wait no more than forty-eight hours* to follow up on a customer problem.

ALERT MANAGEMENT

All professional VoC software platforms have sophisticated alert management capabilities that can streamline your recover alert processes within your organization. Alert management includes workflows that allow alerts to be assigned and reassigned. You can see the number of days each recover alert is outstanding, and whether its status is open, closed, or pending. All notes about the customer issue and its resolution should be housed and accessible within alert management.

Even in a decentralized model, someone in corporate will

likely want to know the number of alerts triggered by a specific location or the current number of open alerts. They should be able to spot key issues and compare locations, allowing them to see how their locations compare.

This is where it becomes important to select the right VoC partner for your situation. Some VoC software providers charge companies on a per-user basis, which can indirectly influence companies to limit the number of people who can access case management. An unlimited user model, on the other hand, encourages people to look at customer feedback more frequently and provides flexibility in assigning alerts to anyone in the organization who is best equipped to follow up on them. At PeopleMetrics, we believe so strongly in the value of a good customer experience that we feature an unlimited user model so that every employee in the organization can participate in creating better customer experiences. That leads to a more customer-centric culture—now that's an idea!

DOES CLOSING THE LOOP PAY?

We've had clients ask us if closing the loop with unhappy customers is worth the effort. *Has fixing the problem really helped them? Were customers retained? Did their NPS score rise?*

In response, we created what we call a *Full Circle Survey*.

Here is how it works: When a recover alert is resolved and closed, we reach back out to the customer with a few questions. We ask, "Did the person who contacted you fully address your concern or resolve your problem?" If the customer's problem was not resolved, we reopen the case. If the customer's problem was resolved, we ask them if their perception of the company improved, stayed the same, or worsened, based on the resolution.

This is a simple follow-up to the original follow-up, and it has yielded a 25% response rate from customers! Since most recover alerts are triggered by detractors, how a company addresses their concerns is extremely important for future business. After this follow-up, 48% of the detractors have said that their perception of the company improved!

The takeaway here is that once a recover alert is closed, the problem still may be out there in the customer's mind. The best practice is to follow up after the alert is closed to find out. If it wasn't resolved, you have an opportunity to make it right. If it was resolved, you can figure out the impact of that extra interaction with the customer and whether it improved the relationship. This technique is not common practice yet, so putting it into practice will give you a leg up on the competition.

CHECKLIST FOR GETTING YOUR ALERTS RIGHT

☐ **Alerts that are generated based on an individual** customer response to a transactional VoC survey is your single biggest source of gold in your VoC program. Mine these alerts very carefully.

☐ **Recover alerts are generated after a customer answers** an item on the survey that deems them "at risk"—usually they indicated that a problem occurred in their most recent experience or they identified themselves as a detractor via NPS.

☐ **You must follow up with customers who generate a recover alert as soon as possible** after receiving it. If you are a B2B business or a high-end B2C business, this means *every* recover alert! If you are a high-volume B2C company, use customer lifetime value (CLV) to help you prioritize follow-up.

☐ **A key decision you will need to make is how you will handle closing the loop** on recover alerts—your choices are a centralized model, which has a group of dedicated people whose job it is to close the loop, or a decentralized model, where the loop closing is handled by the person or team where the experience originated.

☐ **With recover alerts, after your team closes the loop and closes the alert, consider a Full Circle Survey** that reaches out to customers to make sure they feel their issue was resolved and asks them if their perception of the company has improved as a result. This will allow you to not only fix customer issues that remain unresolved but also be able to quantify the impact of closing the loop.

- [ ] **Don't forget about the other types of alerts** that are generated from transactional VoC surveys—namely, recognize and grow alerts.

- [ ] **Recognize alerts are generated when an employee provides an exceptional experience** that a customer values. *Every* employee who gets mentioned in a recognition alert should be thanked by their manager with the actual customer feedback included.

- [ ] **Grow alerts are generated when a customer indicates interest in additional products/services** or is willing to recommend the company to people they know. This is an often forgotten and highly valuable alert type that generates warm leads to your sales team and additional revenue to your company!

- [ ] **Here's a bonus that was not mentioned in this lesson** (see, it pays to read these checklists!): trigger a testimonial alert when a customer is a strong advocate for your company and provides detailed, open-ended feedback. These alerts go to marketing for promotional use in advertising or proposals. Please note that you will need to get the customer's permission to use their comments in your marketing.

- [ ] **Finally, make sure you invest in a professional VoC software platform** that includes alert management to coordinate your loop-closing processes.

NOTES

LESSON #31

★ ★ ★ ★ ★

RUN ROOT CAUSE ANALYSIS (RCA) AFTER EVERY RECOVER ALERT. IT'S A MUST-HAVE—WORTH EVERY PENNY AND ALL THE PAIN.

Setting up a process and using a professional alert management system to continuously follow up with at-risk customers will generate ROI on your VoC investment. There is no doubt that reducing churn one customer at a time is a great reason to invest in VoC. However, if you want an even bigger ROI and reduce the chance of churn across all of your customers, implement root cause analysis (RCA) on each and every recover alert. This sounds like a headache, but it's so worth it!

What is RCA? It's identifying the true root cause of each

recover alert. What you are doing is identifying what is really causing your customers to indicate there was a problem or they are now a detractor. RCA asks, "What was the fundamental issue that caused the customer to not recommend you, have a poor recent experience, or indicate that they may take their business elsewhere?" After running RCA for a few weeks, you'll begin to see patterns emerge, and often a single root cause will stand above the rest.

In our hotel example, maybe a long check-in line is the root cause of 80% of the recover alerts triggered over a specific time period. An additional root cause might be dirty hallways in guest rooms on a specific floor, or showers with low water pressure. RCA looks for the issues that arise again and again.

HOW RCA WORKS

The extra step required for a root cause analysis can powerfully improve ROI. Without help from a VoC partner, though, the task will may look daunting.

Here's how it works at PeopleMetrics. First, we analyze several hundred recover alerts that have been generated over the past few months. We then create five to ten broad, root cause categories that we found are behind most of the recover alerts. Second, we review and refine this list with our client to make sure these categories make sense. Next, we include these root cause categories as "tags" in our alert management system that our clients use to manage their recover alerts. Finally, we require a root cause tag to be chosen before any recover alert can be considered closed by the client. Please see the included image for an example of nine root cause tags for a B2B telecommunications customer.

Root Cause Tags

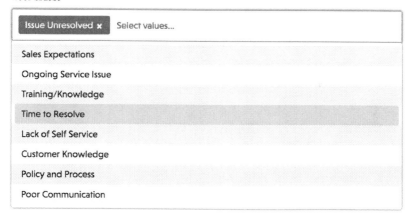

While this sounds simple, it takes discipline to ensure that every single recover alert is coded within one of these RCA categories. And the job is never done. Loop closers must constantly be on the lookout for new root causes. Make sure they don't go on autopilot! They should continue to check their original five to ten root causes and look for any new ones that pop up. For example, maybe the original root cause analysis was run in the winter, but in the summer, problems related to warmer weather services emerge (e.g., an issue with the pool at a hotel). If these RCA categories are not monitored quarterly at the very least, new root causes will be missed.

Categorizing recover alerts with RCA tags is just the beginning. Companies can quantitatively report RCA categories in their VoC software platform. For example, you can now know the root causes of detractors vs. passives. With RCA data properly analyzed, you will be able to identify what we call *systemic issues*—the kind that, if improved, can make a big impact across your entire organization, not just one customer! RCA is a game changer.

CHECKLIST FOR INCLUDING RCA IN YOUR LOOP-CLOSING PROCESS

☐ **Put your ROI hat on**—understand that while saving individual customers after a poor experience via loop closing is a valuable activity, identifying what is causing these poor experiences across the board and fixing that is true scale and leverage!

☐ **I recommend you partner with a company like PeopleMetrics for your initial RCA setup.** This will ensure that you start with the right RCA categories (also called "tags") and that your people understand the process of identifying these tags for each recover alert.

- ☐ **If you want to try the DIY approach to RCA,** the key steps are 1) analyze at least 200 recover alerts so you can identify the top 5–10 categories that are causing these alerts, 2) include these categories within your alert management workflows in your VoC software platform, and 3) train your loop closers on RCA and how to interpret the tags.

- ☐ **No matter which approach** you choose, you must mandate that your loop closers choose an RCA tag with every recover alert before it is considered closed.

- ☐ **RCA is an ongoing process, not an event.** You and your loop closers need to keep an eye out for new root causes that emerge that were not part of your initial RCA categories in setup.

NOTES

LESSON #32

★ ★ ★ ★ ★

COMBINE THE VOICE OF YOUR EMPLOYEES WITH RCA TO DRIVE MASSIVE CHANGE.

The previous lesson introduced the powerful concept of root cause analysis (RCA). The next question is: how do we fix the root causes that are identified? It's sometimes not as simple as it seems. As the head of CX, you don't always have all the answers or even know the best way to get them. Often the best and most effective way to come up with solutions to a specific root cause is by *asking your employees*.

Consider a crowdsourced approach to identifying possible solutions. Research shows that the wisdom of the crowd often delivers either the most accurate answer or the best answer. By involving the whole organization in improving the customer experience, you can change the company culture for the better. People like to know that their voices are heard. Customer-centric culture, anyone?

Fortunately, it's simple to involve employees in this process via a short survey. At PeopleMetrics, we call this process *Associate-Driven Insights*.

The survey should explain that a root cause of many negative customer experiences has been identified. It should describe the root cause in detail, then ask for ideas on how to fix it. There are a couple of ways you can structure this. If you don't have a good handle on how to fix the issue or if you want to get unbiased responses, use the following approach. In the example of a hotel with long checkout lines, the Associate-Driven Insights survey might look something like this:

> "We've identified a root cause of many of our recent recover alerts, and it involves checkout time at our hotels taking too long for guests. Over the past three months, 50% of all recover alerts were caused by this issue via our root cause tagging. Today, guests can check out either in line or using the television in their rooms. Please share any ideas you have on how we can improve this process by speeding it up or completely rethinking it. There are no wrong, bad, or crazy answers; we are looking for any ideas you have. Thank you for your feedback. It means a lot!"

Employees then share their ideas via an open-ended text box in the survey.

Another effective approach, if you require more structure, is to ask employees to provide their top three ideas to improve a given root cause and use open-ended text boxes numbered one, two, and three to gather this feedback.

There is a third approach to Associate Driven Insights. If you and your team have brainstormed possible solutions to the root cause issue, and you would like feedback on which ones make the most sense and/or want to get ideas on how to make your solution even better, you can try the following approach. You might say:

> "We've identified a root cause of many of our recent recover alerts, and it involves checkout time at the hotel taking too long for guests. Over the past three months, 50 percent of all recover alerts were caused by this issue. Today, guests can check out either in line or using the television in their rooms. We've identified three possible solutions to this problem and would like your feedback. The first is putting a kiosk next to the front desk where guests can check out. The second is adding an additional head count during peak checkout times. The third is enabling checkout to occur on our mobile app."

They would then rate or rank each idea and contribute

additional ideas for improvement to any of these ideas. Someone might suggest adding signs so that guests understand that they can check out using the kiosk or providing a quick tutorial on the mobile app. You can add an option in this approach for employees to add any new ideas they have to solve the issue as well. No matter what approach you take, the ideas build upon one another and give you an opportunity to fix an issue that will greatly improve the customer experience going forward.

At PeopleMetrics, we've found that employees are more engaged when they work for companies that they perceive are focused on the customer. No incentive is needed to motivate employees to share their ideas, because they want to contribute and improve the customer experience. It makes them feel good to know they work for an organization that cares about its customers. However, you might also consider publicly recognizing employees who provide the "winning" suggestion. You could offer this person a small cash prize or dinner at a restaurant to raise the ante even more.

One last point on this: employee surveys are typically anonymous. While everyone should have the option to answer your RCA survey anonymously, 99% of employees will add their name because they want credit for their ideas. Remember that we now live in a time where people share their ideas more than they ever have. Whether they are on social media or participating in a company-wide survey like this one, people usually do not mind being linked to their ideas.

CHECKLIST FOR USING THE VOICE OF THE EMPLOYEE TO IDENTIFY ROOT CAUSE SOLUTIONS

☐ **Leverage the wisdom of the crowd** and include your employees' voice in coming up with ideas on how to improve a root cause issue that results in a poor customer experience.

☐ **Make sure you include at least your frontline employees**—the people who are interacting with customers on a regular basis. They're often a forgotten voice that will yield gold.

☐ **You can include employees who are not customer-facing** as well. It's up to you. They will often have excellent ideas as well, although some may be too far removed from the customer to provide ideas that can be implemented.

☐ **Make sure you connect with human resources** before asking employees for feedback. While HR usually focuses on employee morale or engagement surveys, they will appreciate being consulted before this process begins. Getting HR buy-in will make your life easier.

☐ **Before you ask employees for feedback, make sure the root cause issue that's included is widespread** and real. At least three months of root cause tagging is recommended before identifying a specific root cause issue to tackle via this method. You will want to have ample evidence that whatever you ask about is a big pain point for customers.

☐ **Use one of two approaches to gather feedback:** 1) ask for any ideas to solve this issue or ask for employees' top two or three ideas, or 2) present up to three ideas to solve the issue and ask which one is best and how it can be improved/implemented. Please note that with the second option, you should always allow employees to provide additional ideas beyond the ones you suggest.

☐ **Make it fun for everyone involved.** Publicly recognize the employee(s) whose idea was the winner, and provide a small prize for the winning idea (Amazon gift card, gift certificate to movie or dinner).

☐ **Everyone wants a customer-centric culture,** but no one knows what that means. Remember that from earlier in the book? Include the employee voice in improving the customer experience and you will be ahead of 99% of other companies with the same goal.

NOTES

LESSON #33

VOC IS MORE THAN COMPLAINT MANAGEMENT. PAY ATTENTION TO THE NEGATIVE, BUT ALSO LEVERAGE RECOGNITION AND CELEBRATE THE POSITIVE!

It *is* possible for a company to really change their culture with a VoC program. But to do so, VoC has to be more than complaint management. But if you focus only on recover alerts, that's what it will be. To avoid constantly beating down employees with negative feedback, you should leverage positive customer feedback as well.

One way to make sure VoC does not result in a complaint management system is to utilize recognize alerts strategically within your organization. As described in Lesson 30, these alerts acknowledge when an employee does something special or extraordinary to improve the customer experience. Many of our clients manage this by creating a program called the *brand ambassador program*, which recognizes employees who deliver the best customer experiences.

It's easy to identify the employees who are delivering exceptional customer experiences. As you know from Lesson 22, on your transactional VoC survey, you can ask, "Did anybody go out of their way to deliver an exceptional experience for you today?" You can ask the name of the employee or provide a list of names from which the customer can select. Also ask, "What did they do to make your experience special?" This information provides the information that feeds a recognition alert that lets you immediately know when an employee has done something memorable for a customer.

At PeopleMetrics, our Brand Ambassador Awards are reserved for frontline employees who generate the most recognition alerts.

A recognition program based on customer feedback is a powerful way to increase employee engagement and create a customer-centric culture. You're basically connecting the customer experience with employee engagement. Plus, when employees are more engaged, they'll deliver a better customer experience.

PAY IT FORWARD

You can also take this to another level in organizations that have a front stage and a backstage. The people who are facing customers are on the front stage, and they are supported by those backstage. In a law firm, for instance, the partners are front stage, interacting with clients, while the assistants and paralegals are backstage, making those partners successful in the eyes of the client.

One of our clients, Crowe, has taken this front stage and backstage concept to another level with a program they call "Pay It Forward." They use recognize alerts in an extremely innovative way. When a front stage employee at Crowe receives a recognition alert from a client, they then, in turn, can recognize backstage team members who helped them deliver that experience.

PeopleMetrics' VoC software platform automatically makes the pay-it-forward process happen seamlessly. The result is that everyone gets included and feels like a valued part of the team. Ultimately, the front stage and backstage employees are aligned to deliver great customer experience as a team.

When you focus on more than just recover alerts, it improves morale. People buy into the program, and it becomes more successful overall.

CHECKLIST FOR MAKING VOC MORE THAN COMPLAINT MANAGEMENT

- ☐ **You may have started VoC because you want to know about and resolve customer issues** before they result in churn, but there is so much more to leverage with VoC. Don't forget to celebrate success!

- ☐ **Recognition alerts,** the ones that get generated when an employee does something exceptional for a customer, contain gold that many companies ignore.

- ☐ **It is easy and powerful to set up a brand ambassador program,** whereby you simply count the number of recognition alerts generated for each employee and then recognize the one(s) who have delivered the greatest number of them over a period of time. This can be done in the form of a plaque or an award.

- ☐ **If you want to raise your recognition program to another level,** enable your frontline people who are being recognized by customers or clients to then recognize backstage employees who helped them make it happen. Those unsung heroes will appreciate it so much!

- ☐ **Recognizing employees based on direct customer feedback,** no matter how you do it, will result in more engaged employees who—guess what?—will deliver better customer experiences in the future. Customer-centric culture? Check.

- ☐ **You can also analyze the customer comments** on what the employees did to create an exceptional experience and learn successful strategies to improve CX across the board! You might learn that something one employee is doing consistently (e.g., walking a guest to the elevator instead of pointing to it) is something you want to implement throughout your company.

☐ **Customer comments on exceptional employees** who generate recognition alerts also give you and HR a clue as to the type of people you will want to hire. These are also typically the behaviors you want to reward and recognize as heroes in your organization.

NOTES

THE SECRET TO GETTING YOUR PEOPLE TO USE VOC

LESSON #34

★ ★ ★ ★ ★

IF YOU BUILD IT, THEY MIGHT NOT COME.

At this point, you know how important it is to have company executives on board with the launch of a VoC program. You know that you must select the right touch-points, ask the right questions at the right time, and keep a close eye on your survey health. But even if you've done all of these things right, program success is not guaranteed. You're at the end of a marathon, but you haven't crossed the finish line yet.

As important as executive buy-in might be, it's the frontline employees—the operators facing customers every day and representing the company—who must use customer feedback to deliver better experiences. You might build a solid VoC program infrastructure, but that doesn't mean anything unless operators access and take action on customer feedback. Until they are logging in to your VoC software platform every day, reviewing customer feedback and taking action on it, your work is not done.

Think of this as a marketing effort with a requisite marketing plan. Your marketing plan should include taking employees step-by-step through how they will access and view critical results, create dashboards, and close alerts. These training sessions—which can range from webinars to live training—provide everyone's first exposure to the meat of your VoC program. At PeopleMetrics, we frequently use animated videos and YouTube clips to show how our VoC software platform can be accessed and the variety of ways the data can be used. Be creative, have fun, and get your team excited!

By the end of your training, everyone should be ready to log in regularly and review their results. They will be able to track changes, see what their customers are saying, and brainstorm how they're going to fix customer issues. You know what is really happening here, right? Your organization is becoming more customer-centric!

MOTIVATING USAGE

In the beginning, no matter how hard you try, not everyone will be excited about VoC. At PeopleMetrics, to ease folks into the habit of consuming customer feedback regularly, we use what we call *push reports*. A push report is simply a daily or weekly snapshot sent via email or text to anyone who accesses the VoC software platform, with a summary of key results for the week or month. It usually includes NPS, a measure of CX (customer satisfaction or customer effort), different types of alerts generated, and other KPIs. These push reports preview what is in the platform and invite employees to log in to see more. In other words, it's a friendly way to nudge them deeper into VoC.

Once you've established the importance of VoC, one way to make it more compelling is to turn it into a game. Create different expertise levels based on the number of times people log in, the number of alerts they've closed, and the number of dashboards they create. Employees can also advance in the game by sharing dashboards, charts, and graphs created in the program, earning badges based on their activity level in the system.

You can also create fun contests based on VoC program goals. You might reward the highest NPS for a given location for a particular quarter/year, or maybe the company wants each region to reach an NPS of 50, so those who exceed 50 are recognized and receive a prize.

The best part of these competitions is that they ultimately benefit the customer. People are excited to be part of something bigger than themselves, and a successful VoC program helps achieve that company dynamic.

One final word on this important topic: employees are better motivated about VoC when their executive team is excited and motivated as well. We have clients who implement a sort of "walk the talk" exercise, where members of the leadership team are hands-on in helping deliver a better customer experience. For example, we have a client who assigns specific regions to members of the leadership team. These leaders are responsible for their region's NPS score, and they each work with their respective teams to create the best customer experience possible. The executives meet with their teams regularly and brainstorm various ways to improve based on customer feedback. The executives are also accountable for reporting their results (often having their compensation at risk; see the next lesson), so their buy-in goes beyond just talking about the program.

CHECKLIST FOR GETTING YOUR PEOPLE EXCITED ABOUT VOC

☐ **Always, always remember why you were hired**: to help your organization deliver better customer experiences that drive business results like reduction in churn. Print it out, and put it where you can see it every day.

- The only way you can truly do your job is if you get operators to view customer feedback regularly and act on this feedback. There is no other way.
- The people who are acting on customer feedback are most likely *not* you. You must energize your operators to not only access customer feedback but also act on it daily.
- This is the secret to improving CX and increasing your NPS score: consistent action on customer feedback, one customer at a time. The only way this happens is if your people are engaged and working through the customer feedback.
- Do whatever it takes to get your front line excited about VoC. Have training sessions (make it fun), and create contests for people/teams based on VoC metrics (NPS, number of logins, number of dashboards created, etc.).
- Don't expect them to log in right away every day, even if you put together compelling training, fun videos, and great contests. Email pre-created reports or "push reports" to get your front line used to seeing customer feedback on a regular basis. This will whet their appetite on what is available within the full VoC software platform.
- And don't forget to leverage your executive sponsor to help drum up support for VoC. Make sure your sponsor logs in regularly and walks the talk.

NOTES

LESSON #35

THE SECRET TO GETTING YOUR PEOPLE TO USE VOC IS TO TIE COMPENSATION TO THE PROGRAM.

Once you have done your training, created some fun contests based on system usage or NPS, and enlisted your executive sponsor to generate excitement around VoC, it's time to consider the very best way to get your people to use your VoC software platform—tying results to compensation. This is a surefire way to interest employees in VoC.

You can be creative in the ways you tie VoC to compensation, usually through a bonus program. Your bonus program could be based on people achieving a particular NPS level or customer satisfaction score. Another approach is to base bonuses on having a certain number of completed surveys per month/quarter/year or having a low percentage of surveys returned with customer issues. No matter the goal or threshold, if employees reach that target, they are eligible to receive a bonus; if not, they don't. It's simple, it's straightforward, and it's motivating.

A word of caution before going any further: when you are just starting a VoC program, it's best that you establish performance benchmarks *before* you begin a bonus program tied to VoC. Let's say you "believe" an NPS of 40 is a solid threshold to establish a bonus program. You start a transactional VoC survey and realize that all of your locations are at an NPS of 50 or more, and you now owe far more bonuses than your budget allows. It's better to wait. Review your trends. Look at NPS over the course of a year to really see what's happening. After that, you'll be able to set benchmarks and bonus criteria that you can be confident in. Another approach is using a relationship survey to establish your benchmarks for bonus plans in your transactional VoC.

SETTING EFFECTIVE BONUSES

There are many factors to consider when establishing an effective bonus program. For example, are you setting the right goals to encourage the right behavior? Perhaps employees should focus on something other than NPS? And what about your basic survey health? Are you collecting enough customer feedback to define your goals effectively?

B2C companies with thousands or millions of customers, for instance, should make sure that their benchmark goals are based on robust customer feedback. For example, a single hotel can easily serve at least 100 guests a night—that's 700 a week and more than 2,800 a month. With over 33,000 customers a year, you should always have at least 10% or 3,000-plus responses on hand in a given year to make sure that the bonus plan is based on enough volume to deliver accurate results.

Our successful clients at PeopleMetrics tend to be the organizations that tie bonus plans to benchmarks established from at least one year of measurement. They set a budget based on thresholds identified over that year, and they have strong communication with their employees about the program.

Bonus programs do not need to include every employee—in fact, bonuses are typically reserved for the people who are *accountable* for the customer experience. This could be a general manager of a hotel, as well as the manager who oversees an entire region; it could be the head of the contact center or the head of field services. These people can choose to set up a bonus system for their team, but they do so as a separate program. There are usually too many employees for the customer experience leader to manage all individual bonuses tied to VoC.

DON'T FORGET NON-MONETARY REWARDS

Other incentives do not necessarily involve monetary compensation but can be big motivators. Awards and public recognition go far, especially when they're attached to an experience such as a trip or a night out. These incentives are typically connected to programs that are focused on recognition alerts rather than NPS or overall customer satisfaction (see Lesson 33). This is an amazing way to motivate and incentivize the front line!

Stephen R. Covey, author of *The 7 Habits of Highly Effective People: Powerful Lessons in Personal Change*, made a good point: it's possible for something to be *important*, even if it's not *urgent*. Some organizations don't focus on recognition alerts because they're not urgent. In the long run, though, recognition is very important and can yield huge dividends.

CHECKLIST FOR LINKING REWARDS TO YOUR VOC

☐ **The single most effective method for increasing usage and interest in VoC is to tie compensation goals** to key VoC metrics like NPS, customer satisfaction, number of surveys completed, number of problem alerts generated, etc.

☐ *Do not* **create a bonus plan until you have a good understanding of your VoC thresholds,** especially around the metric you will base the bonus program off of. For example, you will ideally need a year of customer feedback before you can be confident in your bonus thresholds.

☐ **You should target your customer-facing managers for your bonus program**—for example, the general manager of a hotel or a manager of a contact center.

☐ **Encourage managers who are part of the official VoC bonus pool to have their own bonus program** for their people—but you should *not* be responsible for this.

☐ **Don't forget about nonmonetary rewards** too—these can be really powerful, especially if they publicly recognize employees.

☐ **Recognition alerts are a great way to include everyone** in a rewards program tied to customer feedback (see Lesson 33).

NOTES

LESSON #36

IF PEOPLE ARE ALREADY USING A CRM, MAKE IT EASY FOR THEM TO VIEW VOC DATA; WITH A TWO-WAY RELATIONSHIP, YOUR USAGE RATES WILL SOAR.

Customer relationship management (CRM) software is common in almost every B2B company and is becoming more prevalent in B2C companies as well. When your company's employees are already utilizing a CRM, like Salesforce or Microsoft Dynamics, your job as CX leader becomes a lot easier. Why not integrate VoC with your CRM to make it easier for employees to access the data they need to better serve the customer?

Here's a simple truth: when employees can easily access VoC, they are more likely to use it and take action. If you integrate VoC into a system that people already use, usage rates will soar. The idea is when an employee logs in to Salesforce to view their customer or prospect information, they can also view customer feedback from VoC.

It sounds great and it is…except there's a catch: often, not everyone within an organization has a CRM license. At up to $2,000 to $3,000 per seat, they're expensive. For example, contact center employees and field technicians may not have access to a CRM, and they're the ones who need to have daily access to VoC.

As an aside, this is one of the reasons we provide unlimited users as our standard option at PeopleMetrics. We do not charge a separate price per user, because we want as many people within an organization to log in to the system as possible, view the customer feedback, understand it, and take action to improve the customer experience.

TYPES OF CRM INTEGRATION

There are two types of CRM integration you should know about.

The first is *application integration*. In its most basic form, an iFrame is used where the VoC platform is given its own tab in the CRM and then some or all VoC activity is done there, creating the "feeling" of a single VoC/CRM platform. The second is *data integration*. The basic form is to utilize your existing CRM data fields and push VoC data to those fields. You can also push your CRM data into your VoC, which makes it easier to send out timely survey invites.

A deeper implementation that combines both application and data integration is to create a custom application within your CRM that can act as an extension of the VoC platform. This is the most work and is expensive but allows for deeper application *and* data integration at the same time.

The rest of this lesson focuses on the basics of data integration and is something all companies should have on their radar.

CRM AND VOC DATA INTEGRATION IN PRACTICE

A common data integration use case in a B2B VoC program is to use the CRM to trigger a survey to clients after an interaction or touchpoint. This makes a CRM extremely valuable to VoC and integration between the two systems a must for most B2B companies.

However, many companies stop there with data integration of CRM and VoC, but with so much valuable information being exchanged, why not make it a two-way street? Moving customer feedback *back into* your CRM so there is a more complete snapshot of the customer the next time they visit is extremely powerful!

Think of it this way: CRM software gathers data about *what* customers did; VoC gathers data about *why they did it*.

Here's the real power of data integration: customer experiences can be *customized* when companies have a record of past actions. If you know that a customer had a previous experience, how it went, if there were any problems, and any steps that were taken to resolve issues, the next time the customer visits, you can use this information to create a better customer experience. For example, if a guest had a bad experience when they checked into a hotel during their last visit, VoC lets hotel management know. A problem alert is generated, and someone follows up, resolving the issue. Then that information can be moved into the hotel's CRM and combined with how much the customer spends annually, the date they first became a customer, and even their magazine and newspaper preference upon arrival. When they check in next time, the front desk will know that they did not have a good experience during their last visit, and they can assure the customer that the hotel will exceed their expectations during this visit. Perhaps a special gift or treat being left in their room is in order.

The key to CRM data integration is discipline. This is,

again, where having a solid VoC partner is helpful. Every detail of the customer experience should not be moved into the CRM. A good partner will know which information is most appropriate to integrate. Also, your VoC partner should understand the IT world and how VoC and CRM systems work together.

Here are a few helpful tips to get you started. Once a survey is completed, create a map of the different fields that make the most sense to move back into the CRM. NPS should almost always be moved, including all the contextual information (i.e., open-ended comments). The customer's rating of their most recent experience is another prime candidate. Anything related to problems the customer experienced is also important to consider including in the CRM. Armed with this information, your front line is in a much better position to deliver a great customer experience the next time this customer visits.

INTEGRATION OF SOCIAL DATA

You may be wondering where social data fits in with CRM; the short answer is that it usually doesn't. Unlike survey data, social commentary is usually anonymous, which makes data integration into a CRM difficult. The only way social data integration is possible is when a company starts a dialogue with a customer who provided feedback on a social review site like TripAdvisor or Yelp. The customer would have to respond to the company with a call or email that will reveal their name and information. Only then could their information be linked into the CRM system.

There are some interesting angles for future CRM integration with social data, however. In previous lessons, we've discussed how customers can be directed to social review sites based on their survey answers. Technically, every customer who completes a survey can be directed to TripAdvisor or a similar social review site. When their survey is connected to their TripAdvisor account, you automatically know their username and identification, and any TripAdvisor reviews can be added to the CRM.

CHECKLIST FOR INTEGRATING VOC WITH CRM

☐ **If you are currently using a CRM,** consider offering some sort of *application integration* so it's easy for your CRM users to access VoC results without logging in to two systems.

☐ **If you are a B2B company,** *data integration* with the CRM is absolutely vital. You will most likely want to trigger your transactional VoC survey based on integrating with your CRM. This is almost always the best way to gather relevant client feedback quickly.

☐ **All companies can leverage true, two-way CRM/ VoC** *data integration* to deliver more personalized experiences to your customers by moving your VOC data into your CRM.

☐ **Use a partner** to make sure you are moving the right VoC data into your CRM so more personalized experiences are possible.

☐ **Unless everyone in your organization has a CRM license** (unlikely given the cost), you will still need a robust stand-alone VoC software platform that everyone within your organization can access.

☐ **The best chance of CRM integration that won't cost you a fortune is to use one of the standard CRM** products like Salesforce. Otherwise, you will likely require custom integration that will likely take your internal IT time or a partner's time.

NOTES

LESSON #37

A MOBILE APP HELPS TO INCREASE USAGE BY EMPLOYEES, BUT NOT IN THE WAY YOU MIGHT THINK.

VoC software platforms are typically full of detailed records, graphs, charts, tables, and lists. Here's the reality: it's hard to make complex data visualization work on a mobile device. This is especially true if you or someone on your team is doing complex analytical tasks. However, you must consider mobile as part of your overall VoC strategy, especially around enabling your customers to provide feedback and your internal users to access and take action on this feedback.

There are two must-haves with regard to mobile and VoC. The first is that your survey *must* be accessible on all mobile devices. This is non-negotiable, and you should insist that your VoC partner provide evidence that their survey renders beautifully on all mobile platforms and devices. As you can see with the two examples shown from PeopleMetrics' VoC, the questions are easy to answer on a smaller device.

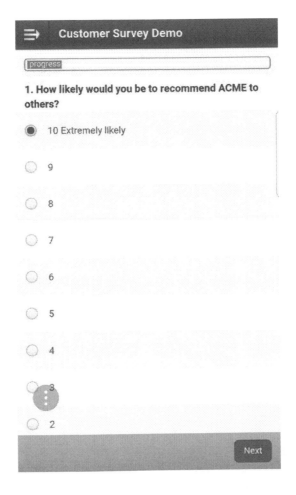

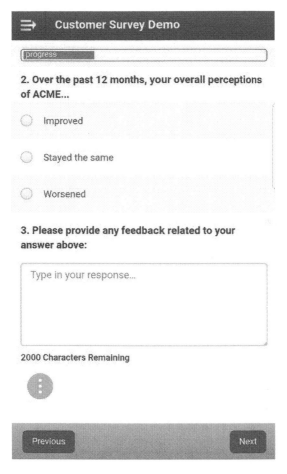

Second, your VoC software platform must have responsive design! This means that whatever renders on your larger screen automatically gets resized for mobile devices. This will allow you to access everything on your mobile device that you could on your computer. The real question is this: *will you want to?*

Take a look at these two images. It is easy to understand

the first image that compares NPS by business units. Consumer finance has more detractors and fewer promoters than the owner services group. However, the second image presents a detailed trend graph comparing overall satisfaction levels over time. This type of dashboard would be much more effective on a larger screen where the user could resize the image, add and remove items, and easily filter by other variables.

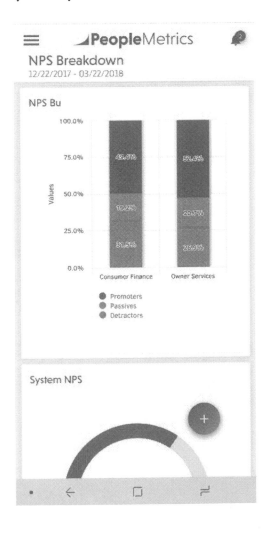

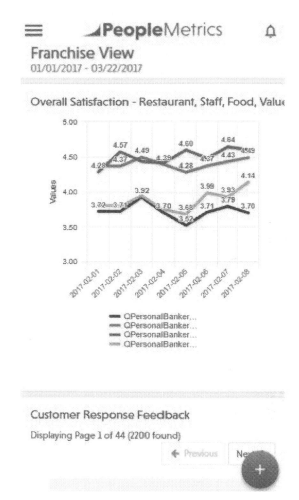

The real issue is that even if your VoC software is fully responsive, employees probably won't use it as much as the desktop version to view more complex reports, graphs, and dashboards.

So, what is the best use for mobile VoC? By far, it's for viewing and responding to recover alerts.

Company operators are prime candidates for using their mobile devices to more effectively "close the loop" on customer problems (see Lesson 30). It's super convenient on a mobile device. When they are alerted to a customer issue, they get a notification on their mobile device and can address it on the spot. They can also close the loop on the issue directly on their phone by identifying the root cause, entering notes about the incident, or reassigning the case if they are not the appropriate person to handle it.

But asking people to continuously scroll down their screen to view detailed charts, tables, and graphs is not practical or reasonable. Executives may want to see a simple NPS chart, but anything more intricate should be viewed on a larger screen.

A nice item to have is a native mobile "app" that is provided by your VoC software provider. Employees download a native app onto their phones and they are ready to go. While these apps do include dashboards that display over-all results, the primary use is still accessing and closing recover alerts. Also, be careful—some VoC providers charge additional fees for access to their app when you can get the same information by simply accessing their main site via a mobile device.

The bottom line is to use mobile to help your operators more effectively close loops. Make it easy for an operator to reassign alerts, identify root causes, and close cases. Strategically think about how your mobile dashboards should look and who will actually access these, if anyone.

CHECKLIST FOR MOBILE VOC

☐ **No matter what, you must have surveys that render on all mobile devices.** That is nonnegotiable, and you must insist that this is the case. Do not leave this to chance.

☐ **The second must-have is that the VoC software that you are using is responsive,** meaning that results automatically fit for the smaller screen of the mobile device.

☐ **The main use of VoC mobile is to make it super easy for your operators to close loops.** Your people should be able to receive alerts on their phones, easily reassign them to others within your organization, identify root causes, update their status, and close them. If your company is a restaurant, a hotel, or providing field services for customers, this is an absolute must.

☐ **Don't expect or even encourage analytical tasks to be done on a mobile device**—often, a larger screen is necessary to see trends and patterns and to draw conclusions from VoC data.

☐ **Your executives may want to have access to a very simple dashboard** via their mobile device that they can check often—one that displays NPS or other key metrics. Make sure this is available and looks great on mobile.

☐ **While downloading a native mobile "app" has its advantages,** including seeing notifications on the app icon on the phone, this can be expensive to deploy for all your people. Make sure the benefits you are receiving are worth the costs. Often, you can get the same information and experience by simply logging in to your provider's VoC platform via the mobile device.

NOTES

SECTION SEVEN

———

THE FUTURE OF VOC

LESSON #38

WHAT'S THE FUTURE OF VOC? MACHINE LEARNING, MACHINE LEARNING, AND MORE MACHINE LEARNING.

The future of VoC is, without a doubt, machine learning. And the future is now. Machine learning, already on full display with the power of text analytics (see Lesson 4), will only become more important as time progresses and it improves. In this lesson, I review two machine learning–based applications that are impacting VoC now and will revolutionize how operators use customer feedback to create better experiences and drive business results.

TEXT ANALYTICS

Earlier in the book (see Lesson 4), I went through the concept of text analytics in detail. A quick reminder: text analytics uses machines to make sense of large amounts of unstructured customer feedback. It groups customer comments into categories or themes, assigns a sentiment score to each, and provides visual displays, usually in the form of word clouds or tables. I pointed out that humans are not as fast at doing this work as the text analytics tools that are available, which already have an accuracy rate of more than 80%. When it reaches 90% or even 95%, text analytics will be a true game changer. To put those numbers into perspective, we're far closer to 95% accuracy with text analytics than we are to the wide adoption of self-driving cars.

Text analytics is mainstream VoC. It's become a requirement for most companies, and once you have it, you can't imagine living without it. Simply put, it's the only way to understand unstructured customer sentiment at scale so you can spot trends and react to them immediately.

MACHINE-BASED INSIGHTS

A key point in this lesson is that machine learning is not just about text analytics and unstructured data. Machines can also help us understand what we need to do next to improve the customer experience using any type of available data and do this at scale. Machines can comb through quantitative customer feedback data and operational data to determine what to focus on next. They can tell us what will yield the biggest return in improving the experience for the customer and reduce the chance of losing customers. This is a complete and total game changer. And I predict this application will have a far bigger impact than text analytics (which has had an enormous impact to date).

Let's take a step back. Currently, operators rely on dashboards to help them figure out what they should do next to improve CX. For example, consider these dashboards (pictured). These are visually appealing and highly flexible in that the user can move the dashboards around, resize them, filter them by almost any available data point, print them, share them, etc.

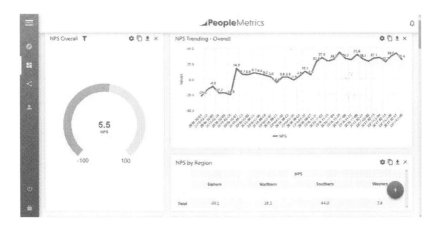

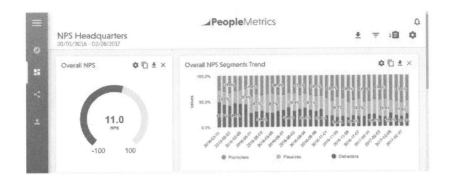

But here's a dirty little secret that your VoC provider probably won't tell you but I will—operators hate dashboards, and many rarely look at them. Most operators also do not like dashboards because they are not data analysts. They have not gone to school to understand data patterns, deep-dive into statistics, or create new dashboards. They simply want to know what happened, in the most coherent way possible, so they can serve their customers better. Also, when employees fail to see value in dashboards, they stop logging in to the VoC software platform, and then you have a big problem.

So, what can be done? Enter offline reports done by a human, usually called an analyst. They tell stories, after all, and who doesn't like a good story? Analysts download the VoC data, use a statistical package like SPSS to identify patterns in the data, and then summarize their findings, usually through a PowerPoint deck. The results typically cover the last quarter, half year, or year, presented with a combination of charts, graphs, and a summary of open-ended comments. Often, they provide recommendations for next steps and inform companies of big problems and opportunities for improvement around CX. Our clients love these reports, because they summarize what is happening with CX and what the client should do next.

But what if you could have the power of an analyst at scale? What if your operators were able to log in and know what they can do today to improve CX? What if they were also provided with specific next steps they could take to improve CX?

Both offline reports and online dashboards will eventually be replaced by intelligent insights via machine learning. This will happen sooner rather than later. In fact, it's happening right now.

At PeopleMetrics, we offer machine-based insights that help operators take the best next action to improve CX and reduce the chance of churn. Using our proprietary algorithms, we examine customer feedback and operational data to recommend next steps. We determine patterns of data that are significantly different based on key measures, such as NPS. We show operators the next steps they should take to improve the customer experience.

Without machine learning, an analyst would need to be assigned to each operator to manually analyze their data. This is ineffective cost-wise and time-wise alike. Ultimately, machine learning will be able to deliver specific recommendations in real time. It's like having an analyst working for each operator and helping them do what's best for the customer every day. And the analyst doesn't get tired and gets more accurate the more data it consumes.

In this image, you can see an example of how machine insights work at a high level. An operator logs in and views their NPS. In this case, the NPS is 25 and they are likely to miss their benchmark target. The operator also sees that their NPS decreased nine points since last month. The natural questions raised are these: why did my score drop, and what can I do to increase it now?

To answer why, the machine learning algorithm identifies which groups have changed meaningfully and why. In this case, the NPS of those who were sixty-five years old or older dropped by twenty points. Coupled with an understanding of which driver was most impactful—a decrease in how safe they felt—the operator has a clear idea of what happened to whom that caused the score to drop.

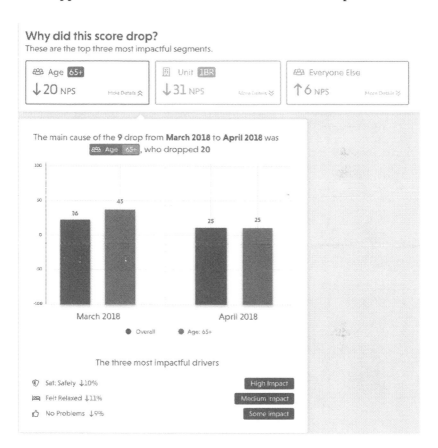

Next, it's time to figure out how to improve NPS! Looking at the top three drivers, the operator would know that what they should focus on now, above all else, is to improve NPS. In this view, the operator would know that overall satisfaction with the most recent experience, that the customer had no problems and felt "relaxed" during their stay, had the biggest impact on NPS. Moreover, the operator can also conduct some simple "what if" scenarios to see how much NPS would actually go up if they improved these items. Let's say an operator has a goal to get NPS over 30. Machine insights can provide the answer to how far the top three drivers have to improve in order to get there. In this case, if the operator improves overall satisfaction with the most recent experience to 73%, those who had no problems to 84% and those who were feeling relaxed to 70%, then overall NPS is expected to increase over 7 points to 32.

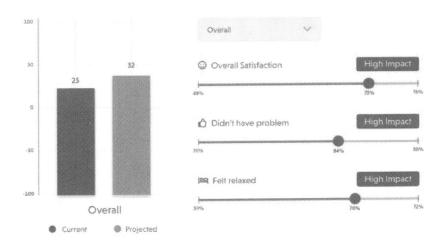

Again, this is a high-level example of the power of machine-based insights. But you can see how much better this is than only providing dashboards to operators and hoping they "figure it out." We are just scratching the surface here, of course. The exciting part is as these models become more sophisticated, the ability for operators to deliver experiences that customers value will only increase!

Another example of machine-based insights comes from fantasy football. Every week, players receive a summary of how their team performed via a story. This summary is really just data and statistics placed into a story about the match with their opponent that week. This same approach is now being applied to VoC; instead of showing an operator a dashboard with the NPS trend and the key problem categories from the past week, a narrative instead describes what is going on in a story form.

An operator may log in to the system to read the following narrative:

> "Welcome back. Since yesterday, it looks like you have five additional promoters but eight additional detractors. You might want to look at that. The major problem since yesterday is that customers are unhappy with the contact center because the wait times are too long. The good news is that you've received twenty recognition alerts. Madeline has received the most recognition alerts because she is going above and beyond to help customers find a restaurant that they love. We look forward to seeing you tomorrow."

This is the analysis of a machine, not a human.

Only our imagination can limit what is possible in the future with machine learning, customer feedback and delivering better customer experiences. One thing is certain: machine learning will very soon have a leading role in all analytical findings—the things your operators will need to know to improve the customer experience. Get on this train or be left behind.

CHECKLIST FOR STARTING YOUR MACHINE LEARNING JOURNEY

☐ **At a minimum, make sure you have text analytics** as a key component of your VoC program.

☐ **Review Lesson 4** for more details on setting up a world-class text analytics program.

☐ **Don't stop there**, though; the real power of machine learning is helping operators know what they need to do next to improve the customer experience and drive business results.

☐ **Shameless plug: contact us at PeopleMetrics** so we can show you how you can use machine insights to provide guidance to your operators every day.

NOTES

LESSON #39

★ ★ ★ ★ ★

CONVERSATIONAL SURVEYS DRIVEN BY TEXT ANALYTICS ARE EXCITING, AND THEY DEMO WELL—BUT TREAD CAREFULLY.

Static surveys have long been the industry standard, but this is changing. The conversational survey is now available, which is more interactive and malleable as the customer progresses through it. Based on the customer's responses, the machine determines the appropriate follow-up questions.

Conversational surveys may be a way to bypass problems presented with the two-question survey discussed in Lesson 24. Major advances in text analytics allow users to drill down into different areas with the customer so that you don't lack information or wonder what you are going to get from the survey.

Let's say your customer starts the survey with an NPS of 1. They explain that housekeeping was horrible because they rarely showed up, and when they did, they did a bad job. The system detects that housekeeping was the main area the customer discussed, and that they had a negative sentiment toward it. The survey's next question would be based completely on that answer, such as "We understand you were disappointed with housekeeping during your visit with us. Please tell us more about that."

Conversational surveys keep progressing in this format, with questions becoming increasingly more tailored to the customer's experience and answers. Based on text analytics and survey logic, conversational surveys are essentially a conversation between the customer and the machine. Customers are asked relevant questions, and their survey experience is completely unique to them.

This sounds great, right? It's certainly impressive in demonstrations. However, like all major advancements, this technology is not without problems.

Because no two conversational surveys are alike, reporting consistent results to those who need it—your operators—becomes a challenge. The answers are usually re-summarized through text analytics and word clouds. This is useful in making quick decisions, but it's difficult to set goals or see trends based on this format since it's always changing. The results are so unstructured that it's impossible to guarantee the front line the data they need to understand their performance.

For now, you can experiment by collecting information from a small pilot to see if the information is valuable. Is there any benefit from the conversational survey? What type of information are you gathering that you're not able to collect with a traditional survey approach?

To ensure consistency in touchpoint data for operators, goal tracking, and trend reports, you'll need to stick with what works—which still means static relationship and transactional surveys. Still, the idea that you should have a conversation with customers rather than a one-way dialogue is powerful, and as a customer experience leader, consider it but tread carefully.

CHECKLIST FOR EVALUATING CONVERSATIONAL SURVEYS

- ☐ **Get a demo of how one works**—you will likely be impressed.
- ☐ **Make sure you understand the trade-offs** with conversational surveys—mainly, you will not be able to guarantee consistent results and metrics to your stakeholders who need to know how they are performing with regard to CX.

☐ **Start slow,** and do a test of how a conversational survey works for you with a representative sample of customers.

☐ **Notice the type of additional insights** you are getting or not getting with this conversational approach. Are your response rates higher or lower? Are your customers more or less likely to abandon the survey? Are you getting enough responses for the key metrics that you are accountable for delivering to your stakeholders?

NOTES

LESSON #40

★ ★ ★ ★ ★

IF YOU CAN GET IN-MOMENT FEEDBACK, YOU MUST. IT WILL CHANGE EVERYTHING.

Your VoC program will completely change when you start collecting feedback from customers *during* their actual experience. Waiting a day, or even a minute, is often too long. If you are capable of collecting in-experience or in-moment feedback, you must. It does not work in all industries, however, and it might not be obvious which industries those are.

The general answer is if you are in a B2C industry, there is a good chance in-moment feedback is appropriate. For example, we've already discussed how car rental companies have kiosks that allow customers to provide feedback while they are waiting in line. Other B2C industries where in-moment feedback is relevant are hotels and restaurants.

But no matter your industry, take some time to brainstorm how you can gather in-moment feedback.

Let's talk about some practical examples. Sometimes you'll see restaurants provide a link at the bottom of their receipt, inviting diners to provide feedback about their experience. If customers decide to click on the link in the first place, they're usually not providing feedback until days later. The much better way is an example I referenced earlier in the book. After a diner finishes a meal, the server provides them with an iPad along with their check so they can provide feedback about their experience. If there is an issue, whoever is managing the restaurant receives an alert and can immediately follow up with the customer before they leave the restaurant. Even more, people often feel more comfortable providing negative feedback on an iPad than directly to another person, so it's a great way to collect honest feedback and resolve any issues.

Here's another key point for hotels around in-moment feedback. The majority of guests who post negative reviews on social review sites like TripAdvisor are doing so *during* their stay. As mentioned in Lesson 29, our hotel clients distribute a short survey twenty-four hours after guests check in so they can understand how the guests feel about their experience at the hotel thus far. If they know about a problem while the guests are still at the hotel, they have a chance of fixing it before the guests share their bad experience with the world via a TripAdvisor review.

Response rates increase dramatically with in-moment feedback, and survey health improves. Fixing the problem on the spot shows the customers that you care about their feedback and their experience. Yet in-moment feedback is used in only a select few industries right now. If it's not in your industry, now is the time to consider it.

In two or three years, I predict most companies will gather in-moment feedback, especially with the increasing prevalence of mobile devices. If customers can provide feedback when they want to—which is normally during an experience rather than after—more of them will opt to provide it. Maybe there will be an app that customers can use in real time to provide instant feedback, or maybe mobile phone technology will advance so that the customer voice is recognized and sent directly to the company. Virtual reality might come into play. The possibilities are endless.

CHECKLIST FOR GETTING IN-MOMENT FEEDBACK

☐ **In-moment feedback is incredibly powerful,** and no matter what industry you are in, you should examine every touchpoint you have with customers and ask yourself this question: "How can we gather feedback from customers during their experience?"

- ☐ **In-moment feedback combined with advanced alert management** allows customer issues to be resolved before the experience ends.
- ☐ **If you are in a B2C industry** like hospitality or restaurants, you absolutely should collect in-moment feedback from your customers.
- ☐ **For sit-down restaurants, providing an iPad with the check** provides an ideal opportunity to gather feedback from guests before they depart.
- ☐ **For hotels, simply sending an "in-stay" survey** twenty-four hours after checking in provides an opportunity for guests to provide feedback to you rather than TripAdvisor.
- ☐ **If feedback is negative** with in-moment surveys, make sure you have a tight, closed-loop process in place to resolve the issue on the spot. This will pay major ROI as it will likely prevent the guest from posting a negative review on a social review site.

NOTES

CONCLUSION

ONE FINAL WORD: PLAY OFFENSE WITH SYSTEMIC CHANGE. IT'S THE MOST POWERFUL ROI OF A VOC PROGRAM.

Big changes—systemic changes—impact every customer. While VoC programs are great for figuring out when a particular customer has an issue so that it can be resolved quickly, the overarching goal is to figure out the root cause of the issue so the experience can be improved for *all* customers in the future. Your time, as head of CX, is best spent focusing on systemic issues that impact the experiences of many customers. Make sure that you have your finger on the pulse of the customer by checking in on individual customer complaints occasionally, but remember that your job is to improve the overall customer experience.

When you start focusing on the big issues that impact the customer experience, you are spending your time wisely.

Remember, it's more important to change the process that is creating the problem than it is for you to follow up on individual customer complaints about that problem! For example, if delivery takes too long, the retailer should figure out a way to deliver the product quicker rather than promise future discounts over and over again. Apologizing and making amends gives a nice touch and can be an important step, but fixing the core issue solves many more problems down the road. Think of this as scaling yourself for the benefit of the organization and the customer.

This is not an easy task and will require you to interact with many different groups within your organization. If your company has a digital experience problem where customers are abandoning your website before purchasing, work with the website team to troubleshoot. If the problem is long wait times when customers call the contact center, roll up your sleeves with the head of the contact center to brainstorm how to get calls in quicker. If you're working in a hotel group and a particular hotel's check-in line is consistently too long, work with the hotel general manager to ensure they hire more people for the front desk or figure out a better process to get guests through more quickly. If customers say your lobbies are unappealing, collaborate with the design team to make them better. When customers complain about rude staff, coordinate with the learning and development team to create training programs around empathy and basic customer service skills.

All this work will be worth your time. Spend your time and energy fixing the big things, the systemic things that will make the customer experience better in the long run. One word of caution: systemic change is hard, and you may need some help to make it happen. An external partner who understands how to create a customer-centric culture and the change required to get there is often well worth it. Kate Feather, Managing Director at CRA (www.crainc. com), specializes in helping companies through systemic change to create customer-centric cultures. I highly recommend Kate to make systemic change a reality.

In the end, don't do this blind. Make sure you follow the clues given by your customers via VoC and especially your RCA results. Customer feedback will tell you where you should focus. Listen to your customers, and both you and the company will be successful. Ignore your customers, and both your career and your company will ultimately die.

SUPER-EXTRA-SPECIAL FINAL CHECKLIST FOR BEING A VOC MASTER

Here are my top ten recommendations via the checklist format to create a world-class VoC program and deliver superior customer experiences.

☐ **Get executive buy-in.** Without that, don't bother listening to customers or anything else that comes with it.

The best way to get executive buy-in is to show them the money! Demonstrate how listening to customers will help reduce churn, increase social review ratings, and provide additional revenue through upselling new products and services. You can also point to how VoC will help increase employee engagement through inexpensive recognition programs based on customer feedback. And fresh customer testimonials are a breeze to get with a comprehensive VoC program. Finally, if you are a smaller company or an entrepreneur, make sure that you have sold yourself on the importance of VoC and are prepared to use this feedback as regularly as your financial results.

☐ **Know where you are in terms of VoC maturity.** If you are just starting out, your path will be very different than if you have had VoC up and running for five or more years. The type of survey you begin with will be different (relationship vs. transactional), your resource requirements will be different, the VoC partner you choose will be different, and the levers you will pull to improve CX will vary.

☐ **Get yourself a great VoC partner who can help you achieve your goals.** Your partner should have software to execute your program *and* the expertise you need, no matter what that is. Expertise can range from helping you get a program off the ground to asking the right questions, touchpoint mapping, designing dashboards, and analyzing results. You have to decide what you need to find the best fit.

- [ ] **Relationship vs. transactional VoC surveys: know the difference.** Relationship surveys, where you survey all of your customers at once, are a great way to kick-start a VoC program, get a baseline of where you are, and understand the competitive landscape. However, transactional surveys are the core of great VoC programs and allow you to truly become customer-centric by filtering customer feedback down to operators who serve customers.
- [ ] **Know NPS well, including its benefits and drawbacks.** It's likely you will need to report on NPS, so embrace this reality. It's a really good measure of your overall relationship with your customers. Get to know this measure inside and out, including how it is calculated and the three segments that result. Also understand that it does not measure the most recent customer experience, and you will need another question (CSAT, customer effort) that does that job.
- [ ] **Map those touchpoints, and find "moments of truth."** No matter where you are with your VoC maturity, take the time on an annual basis to sit down and list all the different ways you interact with customers. With new technologies being introduced regularly, there will no doubt be new ways that customers expect you to be there for them. It's Snapchat and Instagram today— who knows what tomorrow will bring? But don't just list those touchpoints; identify which ones where you are most vulnerable. What are the touchpoints that if

they go wrong, the chances increase that the customer will speak poorly of you or leave you altogether? Those are "moments of truth," and you should make sure you are always measuring these on a regular basis. Think about which touchpoints provide the opportunity for in-moment feedback *and* are moments of truth. Here, you can organize a process where customers are saved before they finish the experience!

☐ **Get your customer list!** No VoC program can work unless you have a regular log of transactions with your customers. It's the heart of any VoC program, and without it, there is no customer feedback and no VoC. You must lean on IT and your VoC partner to make this happen. Automate as much of this back-and-forth with your VoC partner as possible. This is the ultimate bottleneck on almost every VoC program I have been a part of.

☐ **Close those loops; it pays for your VoC program.** What's really different about transactional VoC compared to market research is that you have the opportunity to close the loop on customer issues as soon as you become aware of them via an alert. This is incredibly powerful in that you can directly save a potentially lost customer or one who is ready to vent on a social review site. Make sure you have a robust alert management system in place, and enable your operators to close out alerts on mobile devices and regularly track open cases. Closing the loop in and of itself should reduce customer churn, increase your company's social profile, and easily pay for your VoC program.

☐ **Root cause analysis provides ten times the return on your VoC investment.** Take your loop-closing process to the next level by mandating that your team assign root cause tags to each and every problem alert that gets generated. This process takes only an additional second per alert, but the benefits are amazing. You are able to focus on those systemic issues that are causing many alerts. Fix the problem (i.e., the root cause) rather than the symptom (i.e., the individual customer issue). Your time is very well spent here. Need help fixing the problem? Ask your employees for ideas. PeopleMetrics has a program called Associate Driven Insights that does just that in a systematic and organized manner.

☐ **Embrace machine learning; it's the future and the present of VoC.** Machine learning in VoC is for real; it's happening now, and it is the future. You must embrace machine learning if you are going to lead in this field going forward. Text analytics is the first mainstream offering using machine learning, and this should certainly be part of your VoC program. PeopleMetrics is bringing machine learning to another level by helping operators make sense of complex customer and operational data. Our Machine Insights offering provides recommendations on what operators should do next to improve key measures like NPS and ultimately the customer experience.

NOTES

ABOUT THE AUTHOR

 **SEAN McDADE** has been helping companies optimize customer experiences for over twenty years. He is the founder, CEO, and visionary of PeopleMetrics, a leading provider of Voice of Customer (VoC) software. He holds a PhD in Business Administration and Marketing Science from Temple University and has published eight articles in peer-reviewed scholarly journals. A recipient of *Philadelphia Business Journal*'s 40 Under 40 award, Sean is also an active angel investor in the Philadelphia region. Prior to founding PeopleMetrics, he was practice leader of The Gallup Organization's consulting division. Sean resides in Philadelphia with his wife and two sons.

97034201R00217

Made in the USA
Columbia, SC
12 June 2018